TO MUM AND DAD
This book is for you guys. Thanks for everything.
Having our own kids now has only made us appreciate you more!
Your love and support are a great inspiration.

# The
# HAPPY PEAR

Healthy, easy, delicious food to change your life

## DAVID & STEPHEN FLYNN

Photography by Alistair Richardson

**PENGUIN**

**IRELAND**

PENGUIN IRELAND

Published by the Penguin Group

Penguin Ireland, 25 St Stephen's Green, Dublin 2, Ireland
(a division of Penguin Books Ltd)

Penguin Books Ltd, 80 Strand, London WC2R 0RL, England

Penguin Group (USA) Inc., 375 Hudson Street, New York, New York 10014, USA

Penguin Group (Australia), 707 Collins Street, Melbourne, Victoria 3008, Australia
(a division of Pearson Australia Group Pty Ltd)

Penguin Group (Canada), 90 Eglinton Avenue East, Suite 700, Toronto, Ontario,
Canada M4P 2Y3 (a division of Pearson Penguin Canada Inc.)

Penguin Books India Pvt Ltd, 11 Community Centre,Panchsheel Park, New Delhi – 110 017, India

Penguin Group (NZ), 67 Apollo Drive, Rosedale, Auckland 0632, New Zealand
(a division of Pearson New Zealand Ltd)

Penguin Books (South Africa) (Pty) Ltd, Block D, Rosebank Office Park,
181 Jan Smuts Avenue, Parktown North, Gauteng 2193, South Africa

Penguin Books Ltd, Registered Offices: 80 Strand, London WC2R 0RL, England

www.penguin.com

First published 2014
006

Copyright © David and Stephen Flynn, 2014

Main photography by Alistair Richardson. Copyright © Alistair Richardson, 2014

Additional photographs supplied by:
Alan Rowlette, copyright © Alan Rowlette, 2014
Ruaidhri McCarthy, copyright © Ruaidhri McCarthy, 2014
With thanks for all photography supplied by the friends and family
of David and Stephen Flynn

Set in Populaire, DinPro and Love Ya Like A Sister

Colour Reproduction by TAG Publishing

Printed and bound in Italy by L.E.G.O. S.p.A.

A CIP catalogue record for this book is available from the British Library
ISBN: 978-1-844-88352-3

# CONTENTS

# OUR TWO-MAN FOOD REVOLUTION

I'm Dave (right) and I'm Steve (left), and in this book we hope to inspire you to eat more veg. That is it, plain and simple. We have been eating this way for more than a decade now and have never looked back. We want to share with you our passion for creating really tasty, simple food that is good for your health and pocket.

If you are a meat-eater you may be wondering if this book is only for vegetarians, an inner circle book for the converted. Not at all! The whole thrust of this book is to inspire you to eat more fruit, veg and wholefoods, and to make more meals based around these. After all, no one is going to argue with the most basic of advice: to **EAT MORE VEG!** It's best for us and it does the planet the least harm. But we certainly haven't written our book with the intention of turning anyone into a veggie.

In some ways, we were the least likely people you could have imagined becoming champions of plant-based eating. So if we can be all about our veg then anybody can be!

Growing up we ate a totally standard Irish diet of whatever was put in front of us. We loved barbecues, which were essentially meat fests. There was an instinctive sense that 'real men eat meat', and as teenagers, particularly teenagers who played rugby and did weights, it was all about meat and we ate it by the truckload!

During college we were full-on jocks: we played rugby, chased girls and drank like fish and hadn't a care in the world other than stumbling through exams. Our dreams were all about money, flash cars and lots of beautiful women, as this is what society was telling us was 'living the dream'. We wanted to be millionaires by the time we were thirty, have a private island by forty and private planes by fifty!

After college we weren't sure what to do: we always knew we were going to work together and work for ourselves. We never really had any plan of ever getting a 'real' job. It was 2001, Ireland was booming economically and our generation didn't worry too much about being able to make money. While we were thinking about our next move, we decided to run the Dublin City Marathon. About a month before – after abusing ourselves with drink and partying while inter-railing around Europe – we decided we needed to do a detox (not as fashionable then as it is now). We did some research on Dad's computer and decided to eat porridge for breakfast, swap white bread for brown, cut out processed foods and, most importantly, stop drinking! Though we didn't know it then, this first detox was the start of our personal food revolution.

After all our training and detoxing we did the marathon no prob. It was the end of October and we were feeling good and enjoying the extra money in our pocket from not drinking, so we decided to keep it up till Christmas. Just before Christmas we met all our old school friends to go on the lash. The pints were passed around and we took our first gulp. But something had changed. The drink tasted bad and, more important, drinking alcohol didn't feel quite right, though we weren't sure why. We went home – sober – with our tails between our legs but feeling good that we had done what felt right.

In 2002, having lived our whole lives with everyone asking, 'Are you Steve or Dave?' or 'Which one are you?' we figured it was time to see what it was like going solo. Dave started in South Africa (trying to become a golf pro before deciding he didn't like golf any more and going travelling) and Steve in Vancouver (as a snowboard instructor). Steve ended up living on the floor of a vegetarian's flat for his first week in Canada. At the time, it was like meeting a different species of human! He asked the guy if he could eat the same food as him for a week. Eating so much new stuff – lentils, beans, quinoa, brown rice – was a huge eye-opener.

At the end of the week Steve was sold on this new way of eating. Here he was surrounded by young people wanting to party and rip it up, and he was near obsessed with beans and lentils and vegetarian cooking! He phoned Dave, expecting to get one up on him: 'Dave, guess what? I've decided to be a veggie, I like the idea of thinking about food a bit more.' Lo and behold, in true twin magic, Dave replied, 'That's weird, I decided the same thing this week too!'

Our search for health through food had started and, typically, being competitive, it was all about what we could do next, pushing the limits and seeing how we felt in terms of energy and well-being. We decided to try going vegan to see if this gave us any extra superpowers! A vegan is a vegetarian who, as well as meat and fish, also cuts out dairy products and eggs. We really got up on our high horses and stopped wearing leather and went on with a lot of 'holier than thou' type stuff!

Next we decided to become raw foodists (still eating vegan but nothing being cooked). We did this for about a year and were both super-healthy, but a bit neurotic and obsessed with our diets! We lived separately, still on different continents, in a mixture of organic farms, intentional communities, meditation centres. After all this, by the time we got home in 2004, we were long-haired, vegan, organic, trinket-wearing, herbal-tea-drinking hippies! As we said already, before our adventures we were all about becoming millionaires. Now we were back with a totally different perspective. We were all about happiness, lifestyle, community and health. The weird clothes and long hair were just our way of letting people know we had changed.

While we were away, Steve had started reflecting on how his perspective had changed so much in a few years. The idea of taking over the greengrocer's shop in our home town popped into his head. He thought that we could use it as a platform to try to share some of what we had experienced and our new perspective. After a week back home, he called around to see the owner and, to cut a long story short, within a few months we had bought the shop and the food revolution was on the way!

Our aim was to start our food revolution by making fruit and veg sexy. And we wanted to get involved with our community and drag as many people along for the ride as we possibly could.

Six months into our venture, Steve had a college class reunion. He went along in the little red van that came with the shop. He skipped in, delighted with himself. Most of the lads had become accountants or stockbrokers or worked in banks – all suit-wearing jobs. Steve shows up and one of the lads says, 'Flynner, that story isn't true that you're a greengrocer, is it?' Steve stands there, proud as punch, and he says, 'Yep, it's true, lads – Dave and I are living the dream!'

'What do you mean, you're living the dream? You came here in a little wreck of a van and you sell vegetables!'

It brought home to us how much our perspective had changed: this really was our dream and we were doing something that we loved. And we're delighted that that is still the case. We started with an old-fashioned greengrocer's shop and a clapped-out van. Today we have our main shop and café on Church Road in Greystones, a second café in Shoreline Leisure Centre (also in Greystones), an online shop and our online Happy Heart course. We do classroom health education courses, including our Happy Heart course and cooking demos. We have a sprout and wheatgrass farm, from which we distribute our products around the country, and we thoroughly enjoy being partners in a magical local cherry farm.

We are thirty-four now and neither of us are millionaires or even close. However, we have incredibly rich lives – rich in family, friends, good food, connected to our community and full of purpose and goodwill. When we were younger somebody said to us, 'If you love what you do then you will never work a day in your life.' Happily, we can say that 99% of the time we wake up excited about our work and have such craic doing it.

So that's our story – how we fell in love with a plant-based diet and never looked back! We believe that if you look at food in a whole new way it will be better for your health, better for your pocket and better for the planet. We felt we couldn't write a book that was just a collection of recipes: we wanted to write something with soul, to tell you all about our journey and share our world and some of our passions with you. When it came to choosing what recipes to include, that was tough, but the hundred or so recipes between the covers here will give you a fantastic basis for starting your very own food revolution!

That is it: **GO FORTH AND EAT MORE VEG!**

David Stephen

# USING OUR BOOK

Very often cookery books make a point of high-lighting the handful of recipes with particular healthy eating benefits – such as being dairy- or gluten-free. Since all our stuff is already incredibly good for you, we have to do things the other way around!

The vast majority of our recipes are dairy-, gluten- and sugar-free (in our desserts, cakes and sweet treats we use the various sugar alternatives described later under 'sweeteners' on page 231). Most are vegan-friendly too. We have some smashing dishes designed for our Happy Heart course that minimize fat and so are especially useful if you're watching your weight or cholesterol. And a handful of our recipes contain soy.

So that you can get the best use out of our book, we have come up with our own shorthand symbols that will appear where relevant and let you know what's what if you're watching any of these issues:

CD = contains dairy

CG = contains gluten

CS = contains sweetener

HH = heart healthy

NV = non-vegan

SOY = contains soy

Please go to our Toolkit (page 218) for a guide to some of the ingredients and techniques we use in our cooking and other useful information.

# BREAKFASTS

MMM.....

HEALTHY

KICK
Start
YOUR
DAY

GINGER lemon

# PERFECT PORRIDGE

We couldn't write a breakfast section that didn't champion one of our favourite foods, porridge! This super-nourishing meal can also double up as a lazy, hug-like supper. We usually make our porridge with half rice milk, half water, so that it's rich, sweet and creamy, while being dairy-free and super-wholesome.

There are typically two types of porridge oat flakes available: jumbo oats, which are bigger than regular oats and don't break down as well – they tend to have a bit more bite to them – and regular or standard oat flakes, which are the norm. If you don't know which you have been using, chances are they are standard oat flakes. Pinhead oats are also available, but we usually find them a bit more hard-core in that you need to soak them overnight and even then they still have a bit too much bite to them.

Think of porridge as a blank canvas – it's what you do with it that really makes it. In Dave's house they have a brekkie tray with about ten different porridge toppings on it to choose from. Dave likes to put granola and sugar-free bran flakes on his. Steve likes raisins, banana and honey. It's all a matter of taste and preference. Here is a simple recipe for perfect porridge.

- 1 mug of porridge oats
- 1 mug of rice milk
- 1 mug of water

Put all the ingredients into a medium pan and stir together. The porridge is sweeter if you cook it slowly on a low heat (10–15 minutes). If you don't have time for this, turn the heat up high, stir regularly and it should be done when it starts to bubble (about 5 minutes).

### Toppings to try

granola in all its many shapes and forms • honey • dried mulberries • fresh apple and/or banana • fresh berries – raspberries, blueberries, straw-berries • goji berries • raisins • superfood break-fast mixes • seeds – pumpkin, sunflower, sesame

# MILLET PORRIDGE SERVES 1

A gluten-free and super-wholesome start to the day. Millet is in the same league as quinoa – they are both superfood grains that are great sources of fuel. Millet is very soothing for the digestion and great for nourishing the kidneys, our foundation organ. Use millet flakes to make millet porridge. It is best soaked overnight, as it cooks quicker and tends to be sweeter.

- ½ a mug of millet flakes
- 1 mug of rice milk
- 1 mug of water

Put all the ingredients into a medium pan. Ideally, leave to soak overnight. Then cook slowly on a low heat until it starts to bubble and come together (about 15 minutes).

# NAOMI'S MEGA MUESLI MAKES APPROX. 2KG

We did a detox programme in January, where we prepared breakfast, lunch, dinner and snacks for a week for fifty people. The food was low in fat and all about veg and wholefoods. Naomi (our wonderful cousin who works with us) came up with this muesli, and afterwards people who had taken part kept coming in to buy it.

- 500g jumbo oat flakes
- 375g muesli base (a mix of spelt, rye and barley flakes – available in most health shops)
- 200g sunflower seeds
- 100g sesame seeds
- 120g pumpkin seeds
- 120g desiccated coconut
- 125g goji berries
- 125g chopped dates
- 250g raisins

Put all the ingredients into a large bowl and mix together.

# FRUIT COMPOTE

Fruit compote is a great way to use up a glut of fruit such as apples or other fruit from the garden, or to use up ripe fruit from your fruit bowl. This is our basic recipe (depending on availability, you could use more frozen and less fresh fruit – it's not a rigid recipe). Rhubarb always goes fantastic in compote; it gives a lovely sharp, distinctive bite. If you are feeling fancy, you could maybe add some star anise. This makes enough for a few days, and it will keep for at least a week in your fridge.

- 600g frozen berries
- any available ripe fruit/ rhubarb, chopped small
- a dash of apple juice or water
- 1 teaspoon ground cinnamon
- 4 tablespoons honey, apple concentrate or agave syrup

Put the frozen berries into a medium pot along with the chopped fruit and apple juice and put on a high heat. Bring to the boil, then reduce to a simmer. Add the cinnamon and honey and leave to simmer for 15–20 minutes, or longer if you have time – the longer you leave it the thicker and sweeter your compote will get (it will thicken as it cools too).

Goes great on top of porridge with granola, lovely with pancakes, or even to sweeten a curry!

# FRUIT SALAD WITH SWEET TAHINI SAUCE SERVES 4

For about three months we ate this for probably two meals a day! It is seriously good.

- 1kg fresh fruit, whatever takes your fancy, for example:
- 2 bananas
- 2 kiwis
- 2 apples
- 2 pears
- a handful of grapes
- 1 punnet of berries

**For the dressing**
- 4 tablespoons tahini
- 2 tablespoons honey
- 4 tablespoons oil (olive, rape, coconut, sunflower – whatever oil you like)
- 2 tablespoons freshly squeezed lemon or orange juice
- ¼ teaspoon ground cinnamon (optional)
- a pinch of ground ginger (optional)
- a pinch of sea salt (optional)
- a few tablespoons cold water (optional)

Mix the dressing ingredients together.

Peel and chop the bananas and kiwis. Core the apples and pears and cut into bite-size pieces. Take the grapes off their stalks.

Put all the fruit into a bowl. Stir the dressing, pour it over the fruit, and mix gently.

For all of the following recipes you just put all the ingredients into a blender and whiz together till smooth. Couldn't be easier!

## ZINGY CITRUS CREAM MAKES 1 GLASS

A friend had a version of this when in Iceland, and we have been making it ever since. It will definitely clear the cobwebs and wake you up!

½ a ripe avocado • juice of ½ a lemon • 2 apples, juiced, or 100ml apple juice • 2cm cube of fresh ginger • a few ice cubes

## AVOCADO-TASTIC MAKES 500ML

The creation of our first manager, Sally Marshall, and still a favourite.

½ an avocado • ¼ of a pineapple, skin and core removed • a handful of baby spinach • 350ml apple juice • juice of ½ a lime • a tiny piece of fresh chilli (optional but recommended)

## ELSIE'S OMEGA 3 LIQUID BRAIN FOOD MAKES 800ML

Dave's daughter Elsie loves to make this one, and any variation of it. It is loaded with omega 3s – great for brain function and energy.

2 tablespoons flax seeds • 1 tablespoon cocoa nibs • 1 tablespoon cocoa powder • 3 tablespoons walnuts • 1 tablespoon goji berries • ½ teaspoon spirulina • 6 dried apricots or pitted dates • 600ml apple or carrot juice

## CHOCOLATE ALMOND RECOVERY SMOOTHIE MAKES 700ML

Simple to make, smooth, sweet and packs a punch. Great post-workout. The cocoa nibs give it a nice, almost chocolate chip texture.

4 tablespoons almond butter • 2 bananas • 500ml apple juice • 2 heaped tablespoons cocoa powder • 1 tablespoon cocoa nibs

## CHOCOLATE PROTEIN SMOOTHIE  MAKES 600ML

This is a creamy, chocolatey, nutty, super start to the day. Great for after training.

350ml apple juice • ½ teaspoon spirulina, or hemp or pea protein powder • ½ teaspoon cocoa powder • 2 tablespoons raw cashew nuts or other raw nuts (or unsalted peanut or almond butter) • 1 tablespoon goji berries • 1½ tablespoons linseeds/flax seeds • 1 banana • 150ml rice, almond or oat milk • 1 tablespoon cocoa nibs

# FRESH VEG JUICES

Drinking fresh vegetable juice is the quickest and easiest way to build up your immune system. Because juice has no fibre in it, within 15 minutes all the nutrition has been absorbed into your cells. We like to keep our fresh juices at least 80% veg, and we usually use apple to sweeten and a squeeze of lime or a piece of fresh ginger or turmeric to add another dimension. Some great veg to juice are: pak choi, celery, cucumber, carrot, beetroot, fennel, kale, cabbage, white radish. A good rule of thumb is: the greener the juice, the healthier it is! You can pick up a decent centrifugal juicer for about €100 now. You just feed the veg into the top of your juicer and the liquid goodness pours out into your jug. Drink as soon as possible.

## GREEN MONSTER  MAKES 750ML

1 cucumber • 1 head of celery • a handful of spinach, kale or green cabbage • 2 apples • juice of 1 lime

## VITAMIN C POWER  MAKES 650ML

6 medium carrots • 2 apples • 2 small peeled oranges • juice of ½ a lemon • 1 peeled grapefruit • a large thumb-size piece of fresh ginger

## VEGGIE DETOX  MAKES 650ML

1 medium uncooked beetroot • 4 carrots • ½ a head of celery • ½ a cucumber or ½ a pak choi • 2 apples • juice of ½ a lime • a thumb-size piece of fresh ginger

# SWEET POTATO, SPRING ONION, SPINACH AND GOAT'S CHEESE FRITTATA SERVES 6

Such a lovely breakfast, really gourmet. Served in a pan with some nice toast for a leisurely breakfast, it's a lovely thing altogether!

- 4 sweet potatoes
- 2 tablespoons oil
- 6–8 scallions or 4 spring onions
- 150g baby spinach
- 10 eggs
- 1 teaspoon salt
- 1 teaspoon freshly ground black pepper
- 150g goat's cheese

Preheat the oven to 200°C/400°F/gas mark 6.

Dice the sweet potatoes and put them into a roasting tray. Coat them with 1 tablespoon of oil and season with salt, then roast for 20 minutes. Remove from the oven and either leave it on, or heat up the grill.

Slice the scallions or spring onions. Wilt the spinach in boiling water, then drain very well. Put the remaining oil into a 30cm ovenproof pan and add the scallions or spring onions, sweet potatoes and spinach. Sauté for 5 minutes on a low to medium heat.

Meanwhile, crack the eggs into a bowl and whisk. Add the salt and pepper. Pour the egg mix into the pan of vegetables and cook until the base and sides have set. Then crumble the cheese on top and place the pan in the oven or under the grill until the top sets and turns golden brown – about 5 minutes.

## Frittata alternatives

For a **Spring frittata**, replace these veg with asparagus tips (steamed till tender), leeks (cut into bite-size pieces and sautéed until soft), peas (fresh or frozen – cooked until tender) and finely chopped fresh herbs (e.g. basil and dill), and use either feta or goat's cheese.

For a **Mexican frittata**, replace these veg with a clove of garlic (finely chopped) and a jalapeño pepper (deseeded and finely chopped), sautéed together in oil for 3–5 minutes. Add ½ a tin of cooked black beans (drained and rinsed), a handful of cherry tomatoes (halved), ½ a bunch of spring onions (finely sliced), 3 tablespoons of finely chopped coriander and cook gently for 5 minutes on a low heat. Then add the whisked eggs and a ball of mozzarella or feta cheese. Serve with sour cream or plain yoghurt, fresh coriander, and some hot sauce if desired.

# HAPPY HEART PANCAKES

These are best made small, as if they are large they are too hard to flip. They are dairy-free and sugar-free but they still taste really good!

- 120g wholewheat flour
- ½ teaspoon salt
- 250ml rice milk
- ⅓ of ripe banana
- 4 teaspoons honey
- 1 teaspoon baking powder
- 1½ teaspoons tahini
- oil

Put all the ingredients into a blender or food processor and blend until everything is smooth.

Cover the base of a non-stick frying pan or skillet with the lightest coating of oil imaginable – use a sheet of kitchen paper to mop up any extra (melted coconut oil is a good option). It's just so that your pancake won't stick to the pan.

Put the pan on a high heat and give it a few minutes to heat up. We want a nice hot pan.

Drop in dollops of your pancake mixture and leave them to cook for 3–4 minutes on each side. You'll know they're done when they start to bubble a little and turn golden.

### Some tasty serving ideas

Top with soya yoghurt, fresh fruit or fruit compote and honey, or simply a little lemon and honey. Or try a savoury pancake with hummus, roasted peppers and mixed leaves.

# HAPPY PEAR SCONES MAKES 12

Our scones have evolved over years and have built up a nice following. They are a lovely mid-morning or afternoon treat to have with jam, alongside a nice cup of tea!

- 680g white flour (we use spelt)
- 1 tablespoon baking powder
- ½ tablespoon bread soda/bicarbonate of soda
- 100g white sugar
- 340g salted butter
- a handful of raisins
- 2 eggs
- 240ml buttermilk (keep back a bit for brushing)
- beaten egg or milk, for glazing (optional)

Preheat the oven to 200°C/400°F/gas mark 6.

Sift the flour, baking powder and bread soda/bicarbonate of soda into a large mixing bowl and stir in the sugar.

Dice the butter and rub it into the flour until no lumps remain and the mixture has the consistency of breadcrumbs. Add the raisins. In a separate bowl, lightly beat the eggs into the buttermilk. Make a well in the middle of the flour mix and pour in the egg mixture. Using your fingers, mix to a soft dough.

Flour your work surface and roll out your dough lightly to a thickness of about 3cm. Using a cutter dipped in flour, cut out scone shapes and place them on a lined baking sheet. Glaze with beaten egg or milk if desired.

Bake in the oven for 25–30 minutes, until golden, then leave to cool on a wire rack.

# RYE SOURDOUGH BREAD

The great thing about sourdough bread is that it lasts way better than yeast bread. We usually get close to a week out of this recipe, using no special storage techniques! We like to think of rye sourdough as a very honest bread, really wholesome and nourishing; it has a slightly sour or bitter taste while also having a certain sweetness.

But before you get to making the bread, there's the adventure of making the sourdough (wild yeast, often called leaven) from scratch. For this you need rye flour, water and a jar.

To grow yeast it is very important to use good water. Tap water is chlorinated and is not suitable for this purpose. Therefore, you should use water that's been boiled or is weakly mineralized from the bottle. Filtered water can be used as well. The water shouldn't be cold or too warm. A suitable temperature is about 38°C – do not exceed 40°C, for every degree above might kill the yeast.

Take a handful of flour (about 100g) and put it into a jar. Add lukewarm water a little at a time until you get the consistency of pancake batter. Cover the jar with a cotton or linen cloth and leave in a warm place (25–30°C). Every 12 hours, mix thoroughly, so as to form air bubbles, then cover again and leave. Every day, add about 100g of flour mixed with water to the same consistency as above. Repeat this for 4–5 days.

During this time, the mixture becomes sour and usually begins to bubble. The bubbling may not always be visible (it depends on the bacteria which breed in the mix). After the formation of proper acidity the sourdough calms down.

The smell of yeast varies; sometimes it's a pleasant smell, sometimes less pleasant. But do not panic! When the fermentation process is stabilized, the smell will change: it will be a bit like the smell of fresh cheese, with a bit of citrus oil or balsamic fresh apples.

On the fifth day we have about half a litre of thick, bubbling yeast, which can be used for baking bread. Do not forget to set aside 3–4 tablespoons to use for further baking. Feed the leaven every day with flour and water (as described above).

If you bake once a week you can put the leaven into the fridge for up to 10 days. After that time it has to be fed again. Before feeding, wait until it gets to room temperature. After feeding, leave it for 8–12 hours. Then you can start making bread.

If you use the leaven very rarely and don't want to feed it once a week or every day, you can spread it on baking parchment and let it dry (do not do this in the oven, as it might kill the bacteria). Then crumble it and put into a jar. It can be stored in this form for years. If you want to use it again, just add lukewarm water until you get the consistency of pancake batter.

# TO MAKE THE BREAD

This recipe is simple, and is for the first bread made from the freshly captured leaven.

- 300g leaven (see above)
- 340g whole rye flour (or a mix of different flours)
- 1 level teaspoon salt
- 220–230ml lukewarm (but not too warm) water

Mix the leaven with the flour. Dissolve the salt in a little of the water, then add with the rest of the water to the flour and stir to combine. Let stand for 40 minutes, covered with a damp cloth. Grease a loaf tin with oil and dust with flour.

Transfer the dough to the tin and smooth the surface with a wet spoon. Cover with a damp cloth and leave to rise for 4–8 hours. Wait until it grows to the edges of the tin (the top has to be flat).

Preheat the oven to about 250°C/475°F/gas mark 9. Put the bread into the oven for 15 minutes, then reduce the temperature to 220°C/425°F/gas mark 7 and bake for another 20–30 minutes. The bread is ready when, if removed from the tin and tapped from the bottom, it seems to sound hollow. If it doesn't, bake it for a few minutes longer without the tin, just putting it on the rack of the oven.

Eat at least 12 hours after baking.

# WHOLEMEAL SPELT BREAD

Marius has been baking this bread for the shop for years. It is a staple – a simple, wholesome, satisfying yeast bread that goes great with any type of soup. It stores for a couple of days and freezes very well sliced.

- 500g wholegrain spelt flour
- ½ teaspoon salt
- 1 teaspoon quick-action dried yeast
- 1 teaspoon honey
- 400ml warm water
- 1 tablespoon olive oil

Preheat the oven to 200°C/400°F/gas mark 6. Lightly oil or grease a 450g loaf tin.

Put the flour, salt and yeast into a large bowl and mix together. Dissolve the honey in the warm water and roughly mix into the flour. While the dough is still craggy, add the oil and mix well.

Knead or work the dough for a few minutes, then put into the prepared tin. Cover loosely with clingfilm or a tea towel and leave to rise for about 40–60 minutes in a warm place (an oven heated to 70°C then turned off is ideal if you have nowhere else). The dough needs to double in size.

Bake the loaf for 40–45 minutes. When it's done it will be a rich brown in colour, and when removed from the tin, the loaf will sound hollow when you tap the bottom.

# AVOCADO AND TOMATO TOASTIE

One of our fallback fancy brekkies, easy lunches and lazy dinners! If you are feeling creative, you can introduce any type of pesto, harissa, hummus, mustard . . .

- 2–3 slices of bread
- oil of your choice
- 1 ripe avocado
- 1 ripe tomato
- juice of ½ a lime
- salt and freshly ground black pepper

Toast the bread and drizzle with oil. Split the avocado, remove the stone, and cut the flesh into little squares while it's still in the skin. Squeeze it out of the skin, spreading evenly between the pieces of toast, and spread it out.

Add a slice or two of tomato, a squeeze of lime and a pinch of salt and pepper to each slice of toast. (If you are into garlic, do as Dave does – rub a bit of garlic on to the toast first, and scatter with a few pitted Kalamata olives to finish, though this is not for everyone!)

# CLAIRE'S STUFFED FLATBREADS MAKES 20

The cooked breads freeze well, and rolled thin enough they can be toasted straight from the freezer. The uncooked dough will keep in the fridge for 3–4 days in a plastic lunchbox (make sure the box is at least twice the size of the dough, to allow room for expansion). Twenty minutes before dinner, rip off a lump, roll it out, stuff it and cook it fresh to order – it's really simple. The dough can also be used for pizza bases – roll it thin, add tomato sauce and your toppings, and away you go!

- 700ml lukewarm water
- 2 teaspoons dried yeast
- 1kg white spelt flour
- 500g brown spelt flour
- 2 good tablespoons rapeseed or olive oil
- 1 teaspoon salt
- a little extra oil, for brushing
- unrefined sea salt (such as Maldon), for sprinkling
- freshly ground black pepper, for sprinkling

Put the water into a large mixing bowl and sprinkle in the yeast. Stir, then let it stand for 10–15 minutes until the yeast dissolves and appears to froth a little.

Add the flours, oil and salt and knead for 7–10 minutes, until the dough forms a smooth elastic ball. Put it into a bowl, cover, and leave for an hour or until the dough has doubled in size. Proving time will vary (the colder the room the slower the proving). Or make the dough the day before and let it prove slowly overnight in the fridge in a lunchbox or a bowl covered with clingfilm.

Preheat the oven to 200°C/400°F/gas mark 6.

Lightly flour your worktop, then divide the dough into 20 balls and roll each one out flat until it's about 15cm across. Place your filling in the centre, leaving a couple of centimetres of dough uncovered around the edge. Fold the sides in to meet in the centre. Gently pat or roll (so as not to split it open) until flat and place on a lightly oiled baking tray. Brush lightly with oil and sprinkle with a little sea salt and freshly ground black pepper.

Bake for about 15–20 minutes, or until the base is firm and the flatbread is a light golden colour.

### Suggested fillings

sun-dried tomato pesto • basil pesto or harissa with your favourite cheese • finely diced red onion and lightly toasted cumin seeds •

full of goodness

# SOUP

HEARTY...and...wholesome

# THAI COCONUT, SWEET POTATO AND LEMONGRASS SOUP SERVES 4

One of Dave's fallback easy-to-make soups. A lovely sweet fragrant soup with great full-bodied Thai flavours.

- 2 onions
- 3 cloves of garlic
- 2 carrots
- 1½ fresh red chillies
- ½ a thumb-size piece of fresh ginger
- 1kg sweet potatoes
- 3 tablespoons oil
- 2 stalks of lemongrass
- 2 teaspoons salt
- ½ teaspoon freshly ground black pepper
- juice of 2 limes
- 1.5 litres vegetable stock
- 1 x 400ml tin of coconut milk

Peel and finely dice the onions and garlic, and finely dice the carrots. Deseed the chillies and dice finely. Peel and grate the ginger. Roughly chop the unpeeled sweet potatoes into 2cm pieces.

Pour the oil into a large family-size pan and put on a medium heat. Add the onions and carrots and stir. Cover with a lid, turn the heat to low, and cook gently for 10 minutes, stirring occasionally, until the onions are soft and translucent.

Bruise the lemongrass with the back of your knife to release its flavours and add to the pan with the garlic, ginger and chillies. Cook for 2 minutes. Add the sweet potatoes, stirring to coat them in the spices, then add the salt and black pepper and squeeze in the juice of the limes. Pour in the stock and coconut milk and turn up the heat. Bring to the boil, then reduce to a simmer for 15 minutes.

Remove the pan from the heat. Take out the lemongrass stalks and blend the soup until smooth, using a stick blender. If it seems a little thick, add a little water to reach the desired consistency. Taste, and season with more salt and pepper if needed.

# HEARTY ITALIAN VEG AND WHITE BEAN SOUP SERVES 6

This is a really hearty, chunky soup packed full of flavour – great for strength, power and honesty!

- 3 red onions
- 3 cloves of garlic
- 1 bulb of fennel
- 5 sticks of celery
- 3 carrots
- 2 tablespoons tamari, Bragg Liquid Aminos or soy sauce
- 2½ teaspoons salt
- ½ teaspoon freshly ground black pepper
- 3 tablespoons dried mixed herbs
- 1 potato
- 1 teaspoon fennel seeds
- 1 x 400g tin of butter beans
- 1 x 400g tin of chopped tomatoes
- 2 litres vegetable stock
- 100g baby spinach

Peel and finely chop the onion and garlic and finely chop the fennel. Cut the celery and carrots into small bite-size rounds. Sauté the onions and garlic in 2 tablespoons of tamari and 2 tablespoons of water on a medium heat for 3 minutes, stirring regularly (add another tablespoon of water if it starts to stick).

Add the celery, carrot and fennel to the pan, along with the salt, pepper and herbs, and stir. Grate the unpeeled potato, add to the pan with the fennel seeds, and stir. Reduce the heat to low to medium and cook for 10 minutes, stirring regularly.

Drain and rinse the butter beans and add to the pan with the tomatoes and stock. Bring to the boil, then reduce to a simmer for about 40 minutes, until the vegetables are cooked.

When ready to serve, add the spinach and stir well. It will have wilted by the time you serve it.

# IRISH ROOT VEGETABLE SOUP SERVES 6

**A smooth, sweet and substantial soup. Lovely hints from the white wine, rosemary and parsnip come through too.**

- 1 onion
- 3 cloves of garlic
- ¼ of a celeriac
- 2 carrots
- 2 leeks
- 2 parsnips
- 2 potatoes
- 3 tablespoons oil
- 2 teaspoons salt
- ½ teaspoon freshly ground black pepper
- 3 sprigs of fresh rosemary
- 2 bay leaves
- 4 tablespoons white wine
- 70g kale
- 2.5 litres vegetable stock or water
- juice of ½ a lemon
- 2 tablespoons finely chopped fresh curly parsley

Peel and finely dice the onion, garlic and celeriac. Cut the carrots and leeks into 2cm slices and cut the parsnips and potatoes into bite-size pieces.

Pour the oil into a large family-size pan and put on a medium heat. Add the onion, garlic, celeriac and carrots. Add the with salt and black pepper and stir. Cover with a lid, turn the heat to low, and cook gently for 15 minutes, stirring occasionally, until the onion is soft and translucent.

Add the leeks, parsnips, potatoes, the leaves from the sprigs of rosemary, the bay leaves and the white wine and cook for 5 minutes, stirring a few times to prevent anything sticking to the bottom of the pan.

Remove the tough stems from the kale and roughly shred the leaves into bite-size pieces. Add to the soup with the stock and lemon juice. Bring to the boil, then turn the heat down, cover with a lid and simmer for 20 minutes. Stir in the parsley.

Remove the soup from the heat and blend until smooth, using a stick blender. If it seems a little thick, add a drop of water to reach the desired consistency. Taste, and season with more salt and pepper if needed.

# SHITAKE MUSHROOM AND POT BARLEY BROTH
## SERVES 6

This is a really wholesome soup. We find barley very nourishing and substantial. This soup has an oriental feel to it, and if you have any seaweed, such as kombu or dulse, it would be a great addition. If you don't eat all the soup in one sitting you will need to add water when you want to serve the remainder, as the barley will keep absorbing the liquid.

- 1 onion
- 2 medium carrots
- 3 sticks of celery
- 2 medium leeks
- 240g shitake mushrooms
- 200g pot barley
- 70g red lentils
- 2.5 litres vegetable stock or water
- 6 sprigs of fresh thyme
- 2 bay leaves
- dried seaweed, such as kombu or dulse (optional)
- 5 tablespoons tamari (less if you want it less salty)
- 2 teaspoons salt
- ½ teaspoon ground black pepper
- 1 tablespoon fresh miso (not essential, but it's nice!)

Peel and finely slice the onion, and finely slice the carrots. Finely dice the celery and leeks, green tops included. Wipe the mushrooms and cut them into halves or quarters.

Rinse the barley and lentils and put them into a large family-size pan. Add the stock, stirring occasionally, then put on a high heat and bring to the boil.

Strip the leaves off the thyme sprigs and add to the pan along with the bay leaves. If using any dried seaweed, add it now. Add the onion, carrots and celery and bring back to the boil. Reduce the heat and simmer for 15 minutes.

Add the mushrooms, leeks, tamari, salt and black pepper and simmer for a further 25 minutes.

Check to see that the barley is properly cooked before serving – it should have no real bite to it and the white centre of the grain should be cooked (barley usually takes 40 minutes to cook).

Add the miso to the soup just before serving and stir until it melts in. Season with more salt and pepper if you think it needs it.

# CHUNKY SPANISH LENTIL AND VEG SOUP
## SERVES 6

Walks the line beautifully between a soup and a stew and could form a new category called a stoup! It's a very substantial, hefty soup, perfect with a few hunks of bread and great for when you are hungry and tired. A couple of teaspoons of sun-dried tomato pesto goes great stirred through. It freezes really well.

- 1 onion
- 3 cloves of garlic
- 2 carrots
- 3 sticks of celery
- 2 leeks
- 2 potatoes
- 1 parsnip
- 3 tablespoons oil
- 1 teaspoon salt
- ½ teaspoon freshly ground black pepper
- 3 fresh ripe tomatoes or 1 x 400g tin of chopped tomatoes
- 150g Puy lentils, or other green or brown lentils
- 4 tablespoons tamari
- juice of ½ a lemon
- 2 bay leaves
- 6 sprigs of fresh thyme
- 3 sprigs of fresh rosemary
- 2.5 litres vegetable stock or water
- 100g baby spinach

Peel and finely dice the onion and garlic. Slice the carrots, celery and leeks into 2cm rounds, and cut the potatoes and parsnip into bite-size pieces.

Pour the oil into a large family-size pan and put on a medium heat. Add the onion, celery, garlic, carrots, salt and black pepper and stir. Cover with a lid, turn the heat to low, and cook gently for 15 minutes, until the onion is soft and translucent, stirring occasionally.

Finely dice the tomatoes if using fresh ones. Add the fresh or tinned tomatoes to the pan with the leeks, parsnips, potatoes and lentils, then add the tamari, lemon juice, bay leaves and the leaves from the thyme and rosemary. Pour in the stock, turn the heat up to high, bring to the boil, stirring a few times, then reduce the heat to a simmer for 20 minutes.

Taste to see that the lentils are cooked, and season with more salt and pepper if it needs it.

Just before serving, stir in the spinach.

# BROCCOLI, SWEET POTATO AND GINGER SOUP
## SERVES 4

We have been making this soup for about eight years in the café. Paul Buggle was the first to make it – thank you, Paul! These veg just go really well together.

- 1 onion
- ¼ of a celeriac or 3 sticks of celery
- 3 cloves of garlic
- 1 decent head of broccoli
- 1 carrot
- 300g sweet potatoes
- 2 tablespoons oil
- 2 teaspoons salt
- ½ teaspoon freshly ground black pepper
- 2 teaspoons ground cumin
- 4–5cm piece of fresh ginger
- 1.5 litres vegetable stock or water

Peel and roughly chop the onion, celeriac and garlic. Roughly chop the broccoli florets and cut the stem up nice and small. Roughly chop the carrot and sweet potatoes.

Pour the oil into a large family-size pan and put on a medium heat. Add the onion, carrot, celeriac and garlic and stir. Cover with a lid, then turn the heat to low and cook gently for 15 minutes, stirring occasionally.

Add the broccoli and sweet potatoes along with the salt, black pepper and cumin and cook, stirring, for 3 minutes. Finely grate in the ginger. Add the stock and bring to the boil, then turn down the heat, cover with a lid and simmer for 30 minutes.

Remove the soup from the heat and blend until smooth, using a stick blender. If it seems too thick, add a little water to reach the desired consistency.

Taste, and season with more salt and pepper if it needs it.

# CARROT, CASHEW AND CORIANDER SOUP
## SERVES 4–6

Simple, smooth and sweet. The cashew nuts give this soup a lovely creamy consistency similar to coconut milk.

- 2 onions
- 3 cloves of garlic
- 10 large carrots
- 2 tablespoons oil
- 3 teaspoons salt
- ½ teaspoon freshly ground black pepper
- 1 teaspoon paprika
- juice of 1½ limes
- 200g unsalted cashew nuts
- 2.5 litres vegetable stock or water
- a bunch of fresh coriander

Peel and finely dice the onions and garlic. Cut the carrots into bite-size pieces.

Pour the oil into a large family-size pan and put on a medium heat. Add the onions, garlic, carrots, salt and black pepper and stir. Cover with a lid, then turn the heat to low and cook gently for 15 minutes, stirring occasionally, until the onions are soft and translucent.

Add the paprika, lime juice, cashew nuts and stock. Bring to the boil, then turn the heat down, cover with a lid and simmer for 20 minutes.

Remove the pan from the heat and blend the soup until smooth, using a stick blender. If it seems too thick, add a little water to reach the desired consistency. Taste, and season with more salt and pepper if it needs it.

Roughly chop the coriander and add just before serving.

# CHUNKY MOROCCAN HARIRA SOUP SERVES 6–8

This is great served with some toasted wholemeal pitta breads torn on top and chunks of avocado!

- 1 onion
- 5 cloves of garlic
- 5 carrots
- 2 tablespoons oil
- 2 teaspoons salt
- 1 x 400g tin of chickpeas
- 200g Puy lentils, or other green or brown lentils
- 100g brown basmati rice
- 1 x 400g tin of chopped tomatoes
- 1 teaspoon lemon zest
- juice of ½ a lemon
- ½ teaspoon ground cinnamon or 1 cinnamon stick
- 2 teaspoons paprika
- ½ teaspoon ground turmeric
- ¼ teaspoon chilli powder
- 1 tablespoon ground cumin
- 2 teaspoons ground coriander
- 1 teaspoon freshly ground black pepper
- 2.5 litres vegetable stock or water
- a good bunch of fresh curly or flat-leaf parsley

Peel and finely dice the onion and garlic. Finely slice the carrots. Pour the oil into a large family-size pan and place on a medium heat. Add the onion, garlic, carrots and salt and stir. Cover with a lid, then turn the heat to low and cook gently for 15 minutes, stirring occasionally, until the onions are soft and translucent.

Drain and rinse the chickpeas and add to the pan with the lentils, rice, tomatoes, lemon zest and juice, and all the spices including the black pepper. Pour in the stock, turn the heat to high, bring to the boil, stirring a few times, then reduce the heat to a simmer for 25–30 minutes.

Taste to make sure the lentils and rice are properly cooked. If they are not, let the soup simmer for a bit longer, until they are done.

Taste, and season with more salt and pepper if necessary. Before serving, finely chop the parsley and add to the soup.

# ARMENIAN LENTIL SOUP SERVES 4–6

Such a lovely soup! This is one of the staple soups Dorene makes in the café. It is so easy to eat a couple of bowls of this soup – it is sweet yet substantial and really wholesome.

- 150g red lentils
- 1 onion
- ¼ of a celeriac
- 2 cloves of garlic
- 2 carrots
- 1 medium potato
- 2 tablespoons oil
- 2 teaspoons salt
- ½ teaspoon freshly ground black pepper
- 2.5 litres vegetable stock or water
- 100g dried apricots
- 1 tablespoon ground cumin
- 1 teaspoon dried thyme or a few sprigs of fresh thyme
- juice of ½ a lemon
- a small bunch of fresh coriander, chopped

If possible, soak the lentils for 2 hours before you start to make the soup, then drain before using. No problem if you haven't got time for this – the soup will just take 15 minutes longer to cook.

Peel and roughly chop the onion, celeriac and garlic. Roughly chop the carrots and potato. Pour the oil into a large family-size pan and put on a medium heat. Add the onion, celeriac, garlic, carrots and potato and stir. Cover with a lid, turn the heat to low and cook gently for 15 minutes, stirring occasionally.

Add the stock, dried apricots, cumin, thyme and the drained lentils. Bring to the boil, stirring regularly so the lentils don't stick to the bottom of the pan. Add the salt and pepper. Then turn down the heat, cover with a lid and simmer for 30 minutes, stirring occasionally, until the lentils have turned yellow and the carrots are soft.

Remove the soup from the heat and blend until smooth, using a stick blender. If it seems too thick, add a drop of water to reach the desired consistency. Add the lemon juice.

Check the seasoning and add more salt and pepper if necessary. Stir in the chopped coriander before serving.

# SWEET POTATO AND CHESTNUT MUSHROOM SOUP SERVES 4–6

This is another of Dorene's fantastic soups – a mushroom soup with a twist. The sweet potato, red wine and thyme give it another dimension!

- 2 red onions
- 2 cloves of garlic
- 2 carrots
- 2 sweet potatoes
- 1 stick of celery
- 150g chestnut mushrooms
- 2 tablespoons olive oil
- 6 sprigs of fresh thyme
- 60ml red wine
- 2.5 litres vegetable stock or water
- 1 tablespoon tamari or soy sauce
- salt and freshly ground black pepper

Peel and chop the red onions and garlic. Finely slice the carrots, sweet potatoes, celery and mushrooms.

Heat the oil in a large family-size pan on a low to medium heat. Add the onions and the sprigs of thyme and cook gently for 3 minutes. Add the red wine and allow to cook for another 3 minutes. Now add the garlic, carrots and celery and cook for 5 minutes. Add the sweet potatoes and mushrooms and cook for a further 10 minutes, stirring regularly.

Add the stock and tamari and bring to the boil. Reduce the heat and simmer for 15 minutes, until the veg are fully cooked. Remove the sprigs of thyme and blend the soup with a stick blender.

Taste and season with salt and black pepper before serving.

SOY

# EATING HEALTHY, LIVING HEALTHY

## 'WE MUST BE THE CHANGE
## WE WANT TO SEE IN THE WORLD' GANDHI

As we said in the introduction, we started the Happy Pear with the grand ideal of starting a food revolution, of motivating and inspiring people to eat healthier and be healthier. We were complete idealists and had no vision of what our revolution would look like. We just knew that starting with our little greengrocer's shop was Step One in this mission.

It sounds cheesy, but Gandhi's words really inspired us to encourage people in our community and beyond to take more responsibility for their health. The old expression 'your health is your wealth' has a lot in it: for instance, a study conducted at Duke University, North Carolina, to identify the factors influencing happiness identified health as Number One – without your health, happiness was impossible.

Though we wanted to do something bigger than simply run our greengrocer's shop, we weren't quite sure what that something would be. We finally had our light-bulb moment a couple of years into our adventure when a friend, Maura Winston, said that what made us different was our knowledge about our produce and our contagious passion about it – we really knew what to eat to become healthier and how to prepare food so that it tasted great, and, most important, we really wanted to get the message out there.

Maura was so sure that we were on to something that she asked us to do a cookery demo and education morning in her house and she invited ten friends.

We had no experience of doing a demo, so we were more than a bit jittery. Looking back, we were probably a bit all over the place, but we were delighted to have done it and the response was pretty encouraging!

We then came up with a simple course to be run over four consecutive Wednesday nights. It was a hodge-podge programme – recipes, tastings, information, the latest thinking on nutrition – all to inspire our audience to eat better. We could see that the participants really enjoyed the evenings, as again they were fun and light-hearted and full of tastings. However, we felt people didn't really apply what we were suggesting and didn't make lasting changes. To make meaningful changes they needed to go on something more solid than our enthusiasm and tasty food.

After this we decided we wanted to design a course with more edge. Was there a way of quantifying the improvements to someone's health from attending one of our courses – not just in people feeling more energetic or that their digestion had improved, but an objective measure that could be used to track progress?

We came across research on wholefood plant-based diets that were very effective at reversing heart disease, lowering cholesterol and blood pressure. We knew that this was the road for us. It made sense from a scientific point of view, it was measurable and, being chefs, making the food tasty, attractive and practical was something we would love to do. Out of this our Happy Heart course was born.

We ran our first Happy Heart course with twenty participants picked randomly from those who signed up in our shop. They were men and women and aged from twenty to seventy. The only thing they had in common was that they were keen to improve their health.

We mapped out our course – the science bit, the nutritional information, the food and the recipes and how it all linked up. Local nurses came on the first night to measure cholesterol and weight so that we had baseline figures for everyone.

There was a lot on the line with the course. We worried that if it didn't work it would undermine everything we had invested in the Happy Pear – not just in time and money, but in commitment and belief in what we preached and practised. If our programme made little or no difference to participants, then maybe plant-based nutrition was not as effective as we thought in improving health and

As you can imagine, our nerves were in shreds on the last night of the course as participants lined up to be reassessed. Fortunately it was a fairy-tale perfect ending! The results were fantastic, with the average drop in cholesterol being just over 20% and nearly all participants losing weight. The experiment, the first of its kind in Ireland – carried out by a couple of vegetarian idealists in a greengrocer's shop in Wicklow – showed that plant-based eating delivered!

Over 400 people have attended our classroom Happy Heart courses now and, overall, the average drop in cholesterol is nearly 20%.

After the course got positive press coverage, we were inundated with inquiries from all over the country. However, most people couldn't travel to Greystones and we couldn't travel to them either, so we were a bit stumped, as we wanted to help them. Then David's wife, Janet, had a brainwave – build an online version! Brilliant idea, but of course it was easier said than done. With our typical puppy-dog enthusiasm we figured we could build this in a few weeks and it would only cost a few grand. How wrong we were! It took two years before we had an online version of our classroom course that we were happy with, and it was way more expensive than we originally thought. But now our Happy Heart course was available online to people not just in Wicklow but all over the world. Our dreams of a food revolution had just joined the digital world – a tech start-up from the veg shop! Check it out here: www.happyheartcourse.com. You can read lots of testimonials from people who've gone through the course on the website, but here's the verdict of two world experts in the field of heart health:

*'Twin chefs David and Stephen Flynn have developed a delicious, oil-free plant-based eating program. For those who transition to this lifestyle it will be the end of heart disease, obesity, hypertension, diabetes, stroke, and a host of other common chronic killing diseases. It is a revolution for all.'*

**Dr Caldwell B. Esselstyn, formerly of the Cleveland Clinic, author of** Prevent and Reverse Heart Disease **(and one of the men behind Bill Clinton's move to a plant-based diet!)**

*'The twins, David and Stephen Flynn, chefs by profession, have developed a program that is clearly the future of health and the practice of medicine. It really is an extraordinary story whose time has come.'*

**Dr T. Colin Campbell of Cornell University, co-author of global bestseller** The China Study

# THE COURSE AND WHY IT WORKS ...

Our course is based on bullet-proof science about how to improve heart health. Heart disease is not only completely preventable but in his Lifestyle Heart Trial, the first clinical trial of its kind, Dr Dean Ornish proved that it could be REVERSED in 82% of cases by simply adopting a healthy diet and lifestyle.

If you want to reduce your cholesterol then it makes sense to cut foods that contain cholesterol – pretty rational, right? Foods that contain cholesterol are all animal foods such as meat (white meats too), dairy, fish and eggs. Foods that contain fibre are very important, as fibre helps in the process of expelling cholesterol from our bodies. The more fibre you eat the better. Fibre is plant cellulose, and has no real nutritional benefit other than its prime importance to our digestion. It only comes from plants – from fruit, vegetables, beans, legumes and whole grains – so eating a diet based around plants is going to be very beneficial in lowering cholesterol.

Few will debate us when we ask, 'Who wouldn't benefit from eating more fruit, veg and wholefoods for four weeks?' Well, that's what the course is about. The course excludes all refined and processed foods, such as cakes, snack bars, chocolate, etc., and all oils, as they are high in saturated fat – so that's no olive oil, no coconut oil, no flaxseed oil, no rapeseed oil. NO oil in any form! (See page 224 for more on our views on oil!)

So, yes, it is a pretty extreme diet but hugely effective at preventing and reversing not simply heart disease but also type 2 diabetes and many other conditions. Don't forget this is a short programme to tackle cholesterol and other key aspects of heart health. It is all about putting responsibility for your health back in your hands. These are the basics and the foundation of our health and if we look after these we are less likely to need any wonder drug or cure by surgical intervention.

Once you understand and have experienced the benefits of eating this way, the world of healthy living is your oyster! On the first night of the course virtually all the participants are anxious about what's ahead of them. Afterwards, nearly all say it was a lot easier to do than they had expected.

When you start following the course you might feel a bit peculiar for a while as your system gets used to the new foods and gets over withdrawals from some of your old bad habits, but it's all part of the journey to being a healthier you.

# DO'S & DON'TS TO MAKE YOUR HEART HAPPIER

In terms of health everyone has a spectrum of choices. However, if you are someone who is pretty sick, has high cholesterol and needs to lose weight, it's best to stick to these do's strictly. However, if you have no risk factors for heart disease and you just want to be a little healthier, you might only want to make smaller changes.

## DO'S:

☑ **EAT A WHOLEFOOD PLANT-BASED DIET** – by wholefood we mean any food that is not refined and is in its natural state – all fruits, vegetables, beans, legumes (lentils, etc.).

☑ **EAT WHOLE GRAINS** – whole wheat, brown rice, wholewheat pasta, wholemeal couscous, quinoa, millet, oats, corn, to name a few. When eating bread make sure it is a 100% whole-meal/ wholegrain bread.

☑ SNACK ON ANY FRESH FRUITS, wholemeal crackers with hummus or dried fruit (e.g. dried figs, apricots, mango, prunes, dates, Medjool dates). Dried fruit, in moderation, makes a great sweet snack food.

☑ PROVIDED YOU ARE EATING WHOLEFOODS, eat as much as you like and you will still lose weight if you need to! Because wholefoods are naturally high in fibre and nutrients, while being low in calories, you will feel full and satisfied.

☑ EAT A DIET THAT IS BELOW 10% FAT. By eating a plant-based diet consisting of fruit, veg and wholefoods, the fat content will naturally be below 10%. With packaged goods, ensure you only eat wholefood packaged foods with a fat content below 10%. In general the average Western diet is between 20% and 35% fat. If you really want to reduce cholesterol, eat a diet where only 10% of your calories come from fat.

☑ LEARN HOW TO READ LABELS. That way you can understand what is in your food and determine if it is a wholefood or not, healthy or not.

## DON'TS:

☒ DON'T EAT ANY MEAT – including all red meat, fish, chicken and turkey. All meat contains cholesterol, has virtually no fibre, has saturated fat, has very few vitamins and minerals and will only increase your cholesterol.

☒ DON'T EAT ANY DAIRY PRODUCTS – no butter, milk, cheese, cream, ice cream, goat's milk, goat's butter, etc. Like meat, dairy products contain cholesterol and have no fibre. They are high in saturated fat, so if you do want to reduce cholesterol, avoid eating all dairy products.

☒ DON'T EAT EGGS OF ANY VARIETY. Eggs are high in cholesterol. A large egg has nearly 200mg of cholesterol in it, but the recommended daily intake of cholesterol for a healthy person is no more than 300mg per day. And it's less than 200mg for someone with diabetes or heart disease.

☒ DON'T EAT PROCESSED FOODS – nearly all processed foods contain hidden processed fats, refined sugar and lots of salt. Most of the salt in our diets comes from processed foods and not from the salt shaker.

☒ DON'T USE ANY OIL. See page 224 for our views on oil.

☒ DON'T EAT NUTS. Nuts are extremely healthy but they are high in fat and contain saturated fat which encourages your body to produce more cholesterol, so if you want to reduce your cholesterol as quickly as possible, stop eating nuts until your cholesterol gets to a lower level.

☒ DON'T EAT AVOCADOS – like nuts these are very healthy but they're also high in fat. If you suffer from high cholesterol and want to reduce it as quickly as possible, avoid avocados.

## DON'T EAT ANY MEAT OR ANY DAIRY PRODUCTS

LIKE MEAT, DAIRY PRODUCTS CONTAIN CHOLESTEROL AND HAVE NO FIBRE.
THEY ARE HIGH IN SATURATED FAT, SO IF YOU WANT TO REDUCE CHOLESTEROL,
AVOID EATING ALL MEAT AND DAIRY PRODUCTS.

BURSTING with FLAVOUR
SALADS
fresh and tasty
RIPE
CRUNCHY
be good to yourself

# BEETROOT, SPINACH, APPLE AND TOASTED SEED SALAD SERVES 4 AS A SIDE SALAD

A simple, yet very attractive and tasty purple salad! This is a real staple that we have been making for years. It is very popular and sells out quickly. You can make it a Happy Heart salad very easily – simply swap the oil for apple juice.

- 750g uncooked beetroot
- 60g pumpkin seeds
- 60g sunflower seeds
- 1 large crunchy apple
- 50g baby spinach

**For the dressing**
- 60ml olive oil
- 40ml balsamic vinegar
- 2 teaspoons salt
- 2 tablespoons agave syrup

Remove all dirt from the beetroot, top and tail, then scrub the skin, but don't peel. Grate it into a bowl.

Toast the pumpkin and sunflower seeds in a dry frying pan for a few minutes, until they start to colour and smell lovely.

Core and finely slice the apple and add to the bowl of beetroot along with the toasted seeds and the spinach.

Mix the dressing ingredients in a cup or a jug, using a whisk or a fork, and pour over the salad. It is best to dress only what you are going to eat, as the salad doesn't last so well once dressed.

# ASIAN SPROUTED BEAN SALAD   SERVES ABOUT 6

This is one of our signature salads, loaded with raw antioxidant-rich veggies. It is the dressing that really brings it all together and makes all the super-colourful veg and sprouts jump out and taste so good!

- 4g arame seaweed (optional: this adds depth to the colour)
- 30g sunflower seeds
- 30g sesame seeds
- a handful of fresh or frozen peas (optional)
- 1 medium carrot
- ½ of a medium red cabbage
- 1 red pepper
- 1 yellow pepper
- a handful of sugar snaps
- 1 x 227g pack of beansprouts
- 1 head of pak choi or 100g baby spinach
- 150g sprouted beans (not beansprouts!)

### For the dressing
- a 2cm cube of ginger
- 3 cloves of garlic
- ½ a fresh red chilli
- 5 tablespoons of tamari, Bragg Liquid Aminos or soy sauce
- juice of 1 lemon
- 2 tablespoons honey
- 50ml extra virgin olive oil
- 50ml sunflower oil

If using the seaweed, put it into a bowl and cover with water. Leave for 5 minutes, then drain. Toast the sunflower and sesame seeds in a dry frying pan on a medium heat for a few minutes, until they start to change colour slightly. Thaw frozen peas, if using, in a bowl of hot water for 10 minutes.

Roughly grate the carrot. Cut the cabbage into fine strips. Finely slice the red and yellow peppers and halve the sugar snaps. Rinse the beansprouts and dry in a salad spinner. If using pak choi, finely slice it. Put all these into a large bowl with the sprouted beans, peas (if using), seaweed (if using), baby spinach (if using) and roasted seeds and mix together.

Peel the ginger and garlic, deseed the chilli (or leave the seeds in for more heat!), and whiz in a blender with the rest of the dressing ingredients. Pour over the salad, mix well and enjoy! Once dressed, eat immediately.

# ASIAN BROCCOLI SALAD IN A SWEET CHILLI SAUCE SERVES 4

He Qiang has been making this for many years. It's a lovely fresh, crunchy salad which looks great. The dressing is simple – sweet with a hint of spice.

- 700g broccoli
- 1 red pepper
- 1 x 100g pack of baby corn
- 1 x 227g pack of beansprouts
- 50g sesame seeds
- 60g cashew nuts

**For the dressing**
- 3 cloves of garlic
- 50ml tamari, Bragg Liquid Aminos or soy sauce
- 1 tablespoon paprika
- a pinch of cayenne or chilli powder
- 3 tablespoons honey or agave syrup
- 100ml sesame oil
- juice of 1 lemon

Break the broccoli into very small florets, removing the tough stems. Cut the red pepper into fine strips and roughly chop the baby corn. Rinse the beansprouts and dry them in a salad spinner. Toast the sesame seeds and cashew nuts together in a frying pan for a few minutes until lightly coloured.

Steam the broccoli for 5 minutes, then drain under cold running water. Put it into a large bowl with the rest of the salad ingredients and mix together.

Peel the garlic and whiz in a blender with the rest of the dressing ingredients, then pour over the salad and toss gently. Only dress the amount you are going to eat at any one time, as once dressed it doesn't keep very well.

SOY

# QUINOA GOJI HERBY SALAD   SERVES 4

This is one of He Qiang's staple salads and has a fantastic colour and taste. It keeps really well and is great for lunch the next day. It will be good for up to 4 days if refrigerated. It works great with wholemeal couscous or brown rice too.

- 300g quinoa
- 70g frozen edamame beans or peas
- 50g fresh mint
- 50g fresh flat-leaf parsley
- 30g fresh chives
- 50g mixed salad leaves
- 50g goji berries
- 50g cashew nuts

**For the dressing**
- 80ml tamari
- 100ml olive oil

Cook the quinoa as per the instructions on page 225.

Meanwhile, defrost the edamame beans or peas by putting them into hot water for 5–10 minutes. Finely chop all the herbs.

Whisk the dressing ingredients together, using a fork or a whisk.

Put all the salad ingredients into a large bowl and pour the dressing over them.

# BLACK SESAME, CARROT AND AVOCADO SALAD
## SERVES 4, OR 6 AS A SIDE SALAD

One of Phil's salads. The colours are fantastic and it is really fresh and vibrant. If you can get your hands on them, black sesame seeds really make this salad stand out – they should be available from most health food or good speciality food stores.

- 8 carrots
- juice of 1 lemon
- 1 red pepper
- 2 ripe avocados
- 3 tablespoons sesame seeds
- 2 tablespoons black sesame seeds
- 100g mixed salad leaves

**For the dressing**
- 80ml olive oil
- 40ml apple cider vinegar
- 1 tablespoon honey, maple syrup or agave syrup
- 1½ teaspoons salt

Thoroughly wash the carrots and grate them into a bowl. Add the lemon juice and mix well (this will prevent the carrot oxidizing and going brown). Cut the red pepper into long thin strips and the avocados into small chunks.

Toast all the sesame seeds in a dry pan over a medium heat for a few minutes. When they're ready you'll see the lighter ones darken slightly and get a toasty smell.

To make the dressing, whisk all the ingredients together.

Add the red pepper and sesame seeds to the bowl of carrots and stir in the dressing.

Add the avocado and salad leaves and mix in gently so that the avocado doesn't break up too much.

# CHERMOULA AND HERB COUSCOUS WITH EDAMAME BEANS, CHERRY TOMATOES AND ALMONDS SERVES 4, OR 6 AS A SIDE SALAD

Another of Phil's salads – fantastic colours and lovely musky flavours from the toasted spices. The almonds also give a nice texture. Though they are usually only available frozen, it is worth seeking out edamame beans. If you can't get them, simply use frozen or fresh peas.

- 250g couscous
- 100g edamame beans or peas
- 1 tablespoon coriander seeds
- 2 teaspoons cumin seeds
- 2 teaspoons fennel seeds
- 2 teaspoons sumac
- 2 teaspoons salt
- 200g cherry tomatoes
- 75g whole almonds
- 80g rocket leaves

**For the dressing**
- 2 cloves of garlic
- 40g fresh mint
- 40g chives
- 100ml olive oil
- juice of 1 lemon

Put the couscous into a bowl. Add enough hot water to come just above the level of the couscous, then cover with clingfilm and leave to one side. If using frozen beans or peas, thaw them in a bowl of hot water for 10 minutes.

Toast the coriander, cumin and fennel seeds in a dry pan for a few minutes, until they begin to 'pop' and release their aromas. Grind in a pestle and mortar or a coffee grinder, then add the sumac and salt and set aside.

In the same dry pan, toast the almonds over a medium heat for a few minutes, until they start to colour and smell lovely.

Peel the garlic and roughly chop the mint and chives. Whiz in a blender with the olive oil and lemon juice.

Halve the tomatoes. Put them in a large bowl with the almonds and the drained beans or peas.

Once the couscous has absorbed the water, remove the clingfilm and fluff up the grains with a fork. Add the spices and mix well, then add the dressing and mix again, so that the couscous is fully coated.

Add the couscous to the bowl of tomatoes, almonds and edamame beans, and mix in the rocket.

# THAI RICE NOODLE AND MARINATED TOFU SALAD
## SERVES 4, OR 6 AS A SIDE SALAD

This is one of Claire's salads. It is a really fresh salad that works well for dinner and then as leftovers for lunch the following day. The contrast of the purple radicchio with all the greens really makes this salad jump out of the bowl!

- 500g firm tofu
- 3 tablespoons tamari
- 2 tablespoons honey or agave syrup
- 1 cucumber
- 1 head of pak choi
- 6 scallions or 4 spring onions
- a good bunch of fresh coriander
- 1 head of radicchio
- 200g rice noodles or wholewheat noodles
- 50g sesame seeds

### For the dressing
- 1 clove of garlic
- a 2cm cube of fresh ginger
- 1 large fresh chilli
- zest and juice of 1 lime
- 5 tablespoons rice vinegar
- 6 tablespoons sesame oil
- 2 tablespoons honey, maple syrup or agave syrup
- 5 tablespoons tamari

Cut the tofu into bite-size cubes and put into a bowl. Add 3 tablespoons of tamari and 2 tablespoons of honey or agave syrup and mix gently to coat each piece of tofu. Leave to marinate, ideally for an hour.

Preheat the oven to 200°C/400°F/gas mark 6. Put the tofu into a baking dish with its marinade and bake for 10 minutes.

Cut the cucumber into very fine matchsticks and put into a bowl with a sprinkling of salt. Mix well and set aside. Cut the pak choi into bite-size pieces and finely chop the scallions or spring onions. Finely chop the coriander. Cut the radicchio in half, cut out the end piece and cut into thin strips.

Bring a large pan of water to the boil, add a pinch of salt and the rice noodles and cook as per the instructions on the packet – they should be soft but not sticky. Drain, then cool under running water.

To make the dressing, peel and crush the garlic and peel and finely grate the ginger. Deseed and finely slice the chilli. Put the garlic, ginger and chilli into a bowl, add the rest of the dressing ingredients, and mix together.

Put the noodles into a large bowl and pour the dressing over them, tossing well. Add the tofu, drained cucumber, pak choi, radicchio, scallions or spring onions and coriander and mix everything together.

Before serving, sprinkle with the sesame seeds.

# POMEGRANATE AND GREEN COUSCOUS SALAD
## SERVES 6

This is a sweet and exotic salad, full of fresh herby flavours, caramelized onions and juicy pomegranate seeds.

- 200g couscous
- 1½ teaspoons salt
- ½ teaspoon ground cumin
- 1 red onion
- 8 tablespoons sunflower seeds
- 1 tablespoon balsamic vinegar
- 1 tablespoon honey
- 1 pomegranate
- 30g rocket or any fresh salad leaves
- freshly ground black pepper

**For the herb paste**
- 20g fresh curly parsley
- 20g fresh mint
- 20g fresh coriander
- 150ml apple juice
- juice of ½ a lime

Preheat your oven to 200°C/400°F/gas mark 6.

Put the couscous into a bowl and stir in the salt and cumin. Add 210ml of boiling water, put a lid on the bowl or cover with clingfilm or a plate, and leave for 5 minutes while the couscous soaks up the water.

Peel the red onion and very finely slice lengthways. Mix with the sunflower seeds, balsamic vinegar and honey, then put on a baking sheet and bake in the oven for 15 minutes.

To make the herb paste, put all the fresh herbs into a blender with the apple juice and lime juice and blend until very smooth. Add the paste to the couscous and mix well, until the couscous is green and fluffy.

Cut the pomegranate in half. Put one half face down on a chopping board and gently bang the back until all the seeds have come out. Remove the white pith (which is very bitter) so that only the seeds remain. Do the same with the other pomegranate half.

Add the baked onion and seed mix to the couscous, along with the pomegranate seeds and the rocket, and mix well. Check the seasoning and add more salt, cumin, or black pepper as your tastebuds require!

# HAPPY PEAR HOUSE SALAD WITH PUMPKIN SEED AND PARSLEY PESTO SERVES 4 AS A SIDE SALAD

This is a lovely fresh, light leafy salad that looks fantastic. The dressing is quite sweet and cuts through the bitterness of the radicchio and chicory.

- 1 head of radicchio
- 1 large or 2 small heads of chicory
- 1 x 180g packet of sprouted beans
- 100g baby spinach
- 1 firm ripe pear

### For the dressing
- 100ml olive oil or sunflower oil
- 50g pumpkin seeds
- 20g fresh curly or flat-leaf parsley
- 2 tablespoons honey
- 2 teaspoons apple cider vinegar or balsamic vinegar
- 1 teaspoon salt

Make the dressing first. Use olive oil if you like the taste – sunflower oil will be more neutral in taste. Toast the pumpkin seeds in a dry frying pan over a medium heat for a few minutes, until they start to release their aromas and change colour slightly. Put the seeds into a food processor or blender with all the other dressing ingredients and whiz until smooth.

Cut the radicchio in half, cut out the end and slice into thin strips. Do the same with the chicory and cut into small pieces. Rinse the sprouted beans and spinach. Core the pear and cut into slices. Put all these ingredients into a large bowl and toss with the salad dressing. Only dress what you use, as it doesn't store well – or eat it all in one go!

# KALE, SPROUTED BEANS AND GOJI SALAD
## SERVES 4, OR 6 AS A SIDE SALAD

A total superfood salad that tastes fantastic. With the kale, sprouted beans and goji berries, this salad packs a seriously high antioxidant-rich punch. Raw kale isn't usually that appealing, but Phil's fantastic spicy tahini dressing will make you want more!

- 400g kale
- 3 pinches of salt
- 1 teaspoon lemon juice
- 3 teaspoons extra virgin olive oil
- 200g sprouted bean mix
- 100g sunflower seeds
- 100g goji berries

**For the dressing**
- 1 clove of garlic
- 125ml tahini
- 80g cashew nuts
- 1 tablespoon lemon juice
- ½ teaspoon salt
- 2 teaspoons honey or maple syrup
- 1 teaspoon ground coriander
- 1 teaspoon ground cumin
- 1 teaspoon paprika
- ¼ teaspoon chilli powder
- 2 tablespoons extra virgin olive oil

Remove the kale leaves from the stalks. Chop the leaves roughly with scissors and wash well, then put them into a large bowl. Add the salt, lemon juice and olive oil and massage the kale with your hands for 2–3 minutes. The kale will turn a darker green and the leaves will soften.

Wash the sprouted beans and drain well. Toast the sunflower seeds in a dry frying pan over a medium heat for a few minutes, until they start to brown.

Peel the garlic, then put into a high-speed blender with the rest of the dressing ingredients and blend until smooth. If you don't have a high-speed blender, use a food processor – the mix will be more textured but still perfectly fine. You may need to add a little water to the dressing to loosen it, though it should still be thick.

Add the dressing to the bowl of kale and mix really well. Then stir in the sprouted beans, goji berries and sunflower seeds.

# DRESSINGS

Here are some of our favourite dressing recipes. And of course all the dressings we've given already can be used with other salad combinations too. Tweak things to suit your own tastebuds. When it comes to making a delicious salad the only limit is your imagination!

All the dressings are sufficient to dress a salad for four people. Our method is usually to whiz the ingredients together in a blender or using a stick blender (if garlic or ginger are included, peel and chop them roughly first), but you can easily prepare any of these by hand. Just finely mince or chop any hard ingredients and mix them thoroughly with the remaining ingredients, using a fork or small whisk. The dressings will keep in the fridge for up to a week in an airtight container or jar.

# ITALIAN DRESSING

A fragrant dressing with an Italian twist. Quinoa mixed with roasted courgettes, red peppers and aubergines, with some white beans or chickpeas stirred in along with some sun-dried tomatoes, and coated with this dressing, makes a delicious alternative salad – incredibly satisfying! Nutritional yeast is a tasty vegan flaked yeast, available in most healthfood shops, that is high in vitamin B12 and other nutrients. It has a lovely cheese-like taste and adds great depth to a dish.

2 cloves of garlic • 60ml red wine vinegar • 1 tablespoon Dijon mustard • ½ teaspoon dried oregano, rosemary or thyme – whatever you have to hand! • ½ teaspoon dried basil • ½ tablespoon agave syrup • 60ml water • 1 tablespoon nutritional yeast • ¼ teaspoon freshly ground black pepper • ¼ teaspoon sea salt

# BALSAMIC VINAIGRETTE

A simple classic without the oil! Sure to liven up your salad leaf of choice; delicious mixed with grilled, roasted or even fresh pears and figs.

½ a clove of garlic (optional) • 2½ tablespoons balsamic, white or red wine vinegar • 2 tablespoons apple cider vinegar • 1 teaspoon Dijon mustard or regular mustard • 2 tablespoons maple syrup • ¼ teaspoon sea salt • freshly ground black pepper, to taste • 2 tablespoons water

# ASIAN ORANGE GINGER DRESSING

A wonderful dressing that works well over noodles and stir-fried veggies.

190ml 100% pure orange juice • 80ml 100% pure apple juice • 1 tablespoon apple cider vinegar • 1 tablespoon minced fresh ginger • 1 tablespoon fresh lime juice • ¼ teaspoon chilli powder (optional) • ¼ teaspoon sea salt

# TAHINI ORANGE DRESSING

A lovely fresh citrusy dressing with the full flavour of tahini to mellow it.

100ml olive oil • 1 tablespoon honey or agave syrup • 1 tablespoon apple cider vinegar • zest of 1 orange • juice of ½ an orange • 1 tablespoon tahini • ½ teaspoon salt • 1 teaspoon wholegrain mustard • 2 teaspoons toasted cumin seeds

Omit the cumin seeds initially. Once everything else is blended, add the seeds and pulse briefly to combine.

# MINT AND BASIL DRESSING

Goes well on a simple green salad. Or over some fresh tomatoes and mozzarella cheese. Works well with most combinations of leafy herbs.

75ml olive oil • 75ml unrefined sunflower oil • 25ml lemon juice • leaves from 5 sprigs of fresh mint • leaves from 3 sprigs of basil • ½ teaspoon salt

# SWEET LEMON DRESSING

A sweet tangy dressing – so light and refreshing! It works with pretty much anything, though one of our favourite ways to use it is over roasted cauliflower mixed with wholegrain pasta, spinach and olives. Sprinkle with a few toasted wholemeal breadcrumbs for a delicious midday or evening meal.

1 clove of garlic • 60ml lemon juice • 60ml unsweetened apple juice • 60ml water • 2½ teaspoons Dijon mustard • ¼ teaspoon sea salt • grated zest of 1 lemon • freshly ground black pepper, to taste • ½ tablespoon agave syrup

# PEANUT AND CHILLI DRESSING

A spicy peanut dressing, great for Asian type salads or crunchy greens.

2 cloves of garlic • 150ml unrefined sunflower oil • ½ a fresh red chilli • 1 tablespoon apple concentrate, honey or agave syrup • 3 tablespoons peanut butter • ½ teaspoon salt • 2 teaspoons tamari, Bragg Liquid Aminos or soy sauce • 2 teaspoons grated ginger • 2 teaspoons lime juice • 1 teaspoon sesame oil • 100–150ml water

If the dressing is a bit thick, add more water to thin it out.

# CREAMY CURRY YOGHURT DRESSING

A delicious, creamy, heart-healthy dressing with a bit of a kick. Drizzle this over your salad, or mix it with mashed chickpeas for an alternative sandwich filling. Think curried egg salad – without the egg! Or stir through wholegrain pasta with your favourite roasted or sautéed veggies to make a wonderful salad.

2 small cloves of garlic • 180g dairy-free yoghurt • 60ml low-fat coconut milk • 2 tablespoons finely chopped red onion • 4 teaspoons curry powder • 2 teaspoons honey, agave syrup or maple syrup • 1 teaspoon freshly grated ginger • ¼ teaspoon sea salt • 1 tablespoon lemon juice

# DIPS

## HAPPY PEAR HUMMUS  MAKES ABOUT 500G

This is our take on this fantastic dip/spread. We have been making hummus every day for the past ten years in so many different variations. Hummus is a very personal thing, with some people preferring it with lots of tahini and others with lots of lemon. Texture preferences can also vary wildly, from super-smooth to chunky and anywhere in between. Customize it how you best like it – if you don't know yet, this recipe is a great place to start!

4 cloves of garlic • 2 x 400g tins of chickpeas • 130ml lemon juice (juice of 2–3 lemons) • 4 tablespoons light tahini • 2 teaspoons salt • a pinch of freshly ground black pepper • a pinch of ground cumin • 7–8 tablespoons water

Peel the garlic, drain and rinse the chickpeas, then put all the ingredients into a food processor and blend until you reach the desired texture (reasonably smooth). Taste and add more lemon juice or adjust the other seasonings if necessary.

Serve with toasted pitta, falafel with harissa, alfalfa ... or simply eat off a spoon or with raw carrots!

## ROASTED CARROT HUMMUS  MAKES ABOUT 600G

This is real good – one of Phil's creations, sweet and savoury and hard to beat. Goes great on top of the beetroot burgers (page 130).

400g carrots • ½ x 400g tin of chickpeas • 1 clove of garlic • 4 tablespoons olive oil • a pinch of salt and freshly ground black pepper • juice of ½ a lemon • 2 tablespoons tahini • 1 teaspoon ground cumin

Preheat the oven to 200°C/400°F/gas mark 6. Cut the carrots into bite-size pieces, put them on a baking tray and roast them in the oven for 25 minutes.

Drain the chickpeas and rinse thoroughly. Peel and finely chop the garlic. Put all the ingredients into a blender and blend until smooth, adding a little water if necessary. Check the seasoning and add more salt and pepper if necessary.

Best ever Roasted carrot hummus

WILD·

SWEET and SAVOURY

MASSIVE flavour

generous sq

Coriander pesto

ld favourite. HAPPY PEA

Hea

stalks and all!

~RLIC·PESTO

sweet

CARAMELIZED RED ONION HUMMUS

ezt of LIME

a pinch of cumin

SHINY, tasty and sweet

~UMMUS

Garlic LIME

GUACAMOLE

DIP away!

bursting with flavour

# CARAMELIZED RED ONION HUMMUS  MAKES ABOUT 600G

Skinny, tasty, sweet hummus with a hint of red going through it – what's not to like! Being oil- and tahini-free makes it super-low in calories, yet it punches above its weight compared to other dips. We have been making this for a few years on our Happy Heart course, so it has been tested by hundreds of people.

1 red onion • 1 tablespoon honey • 4 cloves of garlic • 2 x 400g tins of chickpeas • juice of 2 limes • 8 tablespoons water • 2 teaspoons salt • a pinch each of ground cumin and cayenne pepper (optional)

Preheat the oven to 200°C/400°F/gas mark 6.

Peel and finely chop the red onion. Put it on a roasting tray, mix it with the honey and bake in the oven for 20 minutes.

Peel the garlic. Drain the chickpeas and rinse them. Put them into a food processor or blender with all the other ingredients, except the onion, and whiz until you get a smooth texture.

Once the onions have baked, add them to the hummus and blend in the food processor to make a very tasty spread. It goes great on bread, pittas and crackers, and it's lovely with carrot sticks and other crunchy veg.

# HAPPY PEAR GUACAMOLE  MAKES ABOUT 700G

We love guacamole and could eat kilos of it at a go! It is so good and flavoursome, and it also looks incredibly moreish with all its great colours and textures. Like hummus, guacamole is a personal thing – this is our take on it, which we hope brings you as much joy as it does us!

4 ripe avocados (ripe but not bruised!) • 2 limes • 2 cloves of garlic • ½ a medium red onion • 5 cherry tomatoes • ¾ teaspoon ground cumin • ½ teaspoon salt • a pinch of chilli powder • a pinch of freshly ground black pepper • a small bunch of fresh coriander

Halve the avocados and take out the stones, then slice them crosswise into little squares while still in their skins. Spoon out the avocado flesh and pop it into a bowl. Squeeze in the lime juice.

Peel and finely dice the garlic and red onion and slice and dice the cherry tomatoes. Add both to the bowl. Add the cumin, salt, chilli powder and black pepper. Chop the coriander and add that too. Taking a fork, mix all the ingredients together, mashing out any large chunks. Enjoy!

# WILD GARLIC PESTO   MAKES ABOUT 500G

Wild garlic is only really available in springtime, when you can smell it as you walk through the woods. It is not usually available in shops (though it is becoming a little more so than it used to be), so you will probably have to go pick it yourself from riverbanks or marshy woods! Use rocket if you can't find wild garlic.

100g walnuts • 200g wild garlic • 1½ limes • 250ml sunflower oil • 1 tablespoon salt

Preheat the oven to 200°C/400°F/gas mark 6.

Put the walnuts on a baking tray and bake in the oven for 10 minutes. Wash the wild garlic thoroughly.

Put the roasted walnuts into a food processor or blender. Add the wild garlic, stalks and all, then squeeze in the lime juice, and add the oil and salt. Blend everything together till smooth, then taste and adjust the seasoning if necessary.

This goes great with bread and crackers or stirred through pasta.

# CORIANDER PESTO   MAKES ABOUT 350G

Less common than other pestos but equally good, this contributes massive flavour to anything you add it to. Great as a dip, on crackers, with pittas or even stirred through rice! We love it on top of roasted potato wedges.

3 cloves of garlic • 50g fresh coriander, including stalks • 2 teaspoons salt • juice of ½ a lime • 100g cashew nuts • 150ml sunflower oil

Peel the garlic, then put it into a blender with the rest of the ingredients and whiz until smooth.

MAINS

# HAPPY PEAR DAHL SERVES 4

Dahl is one of the most widely eaten dishes in the world – well, in India anyway! A delicious, smooth, lentil-based curry that melts in your mouth, it's like a hug on a cold day and is definitely comforting.

We have been making dahl for years. It's a real staple on the Happy Pear menu most weeks in some form, whether made with red lentils, with mung beans, with coconut milk or without, oven-baked or cooked in a pan. We have never had a standard dahl recipe, and the jury is out as to who makes the best dahl – Steve, Dorene, Phil, David, Claire? There are so many ways to get from A to Dahl!

This recipe is easy to follow and is a good basis to start with. As it's a recipe from our Happy Heart course it's low in fat, high in fibre and full of heart-healthy nutrition. If you are feeling adventurous, there are suggestions on how to pimp up your dahl at the end of this recipe.

500g red lentils • 2 red onions • 3 cloves of garlic • ½ a thumb-size piece of ginger • 1 courgette • 4 medium tomatoes (ideally nice and ripe) • 3 teaspoons salt (use a decent unrefined sea salt such as Maldon) • 2 teaspoons ground cumin • a pinch of cayenne pepper • 1 teaspoon ground turmeric • 3 teaspoons medium curry powder • 1 teaspoon freshly ground black pepper • 3 tablespoons tamari, Bragg Liquid Aminos or soy sauce • juice of 1 lime • a small bunch of fresh coriander

If you have time, you can soak the lentils in cold water for a few hours, but this is not essential. Drain and rinse them before using.

Peel and finely slice the onions, garlic and ginger. Cut the courgette into bite-size pieces and roughly chop the tomatoes.

Sauté the onions, garlic and ginger in 4 tablespoons of water in a large pan on a high heat for 5 minutes. Stir regularly, adding more water if they start to stick to the bottom of the pan. When the onions are soft, add the courgette, tomatoes and 1 teaspoon of the salt. Cover the pan and cook gently over a low heat for 5–10 minutes, stirring occasionally. If you have time, cook the veg for longer – the longer you cook them, the more flavourful your dahl will be.

Add the lentils, spices, tamari, lime juice, the remaining salt and 2 litres of water, and bring to the boil. Reduce to a low heat and simmer for 25 minutes, or until you are happy with the texture of the dahl. Stir regularly, as lentils have a tendency to stick.

Finely chop the coriander and sprinkle over the dahl. Serve with brown rice or toasted wholemeal pitta breads, cut into soldiers. Mango chutney is also a nice accompaniment.

### Pimping up your dahl!

Add raisins and apple to sweeten it. The raisins give a nice contrasting colour.

Baby spinach is great for colour and adds another texture.

For a fresh accompaniment, make a simple Indian salad of finely diced red onion, tomato, cucumber and mint, with lemon juice and chopped fresh coriander.

For a depth of richness to your dahl, add a tin of low-fat coconut milk when putting in the lentils.

# FALAFELS WITH RED PEPPER RELISH SERVES 4

This is a very tasty and delicious recipe, one that kids and teenagers love. It's easy to make and the mix will keep for 3 days in the fridge. We usually make the mix into burger-shaped patties and serve one per person, but sometimes we make it into small bite-size balls – they end up crispier when smaller!

500g sweet potatoes • 3 cloves of garlic • 1 x 400g tin of chickpeas • juice of 1 lemon • 2 teaspoons ground cumin • 2 teaspoons ground coriander • 1 teaspoon paprika • a pinch of cayenne pepper or chilli powder (if you like it hot, add ½ teaspoon cayenne) • ½ teaspoon freshly ground black pepper • 2 teaspoons salt • 2 tablespoons tamari, Bragg Liquid Aminos or soy sauce • 10–12 scallions or 6 spring onions • 1 small red onion • 1 small bunch of fresh parsley • 1 small bunch of fresh coriander • 3 teaspoons cumin seeds • 2 tablespoons sesame seeds
**For the red pepper relish** • 1 medium onion • 2 red peppers • 1 x 400g tin of chopped tomatoes • 2 tablespoons apple cider vinegar or any white vinegar • 1 tablespoon agave syrup or honey • ¼ teaspoon chilli powder • 1 teaspoon salt • ½ teaspoon freshly ground black pepper

Preheat the oven to 200°C/400°F/gas mark 6.

Cut the sweet potatoes into bite-size pieces (no need to peel them). Peel and finely chop the onion (for the relish), and deseed and roughly chop the red peppers. Peel and finely slice the garlic. Drain the chickpeas and rinse them thoroughly.

Put the sweet potatoes on one baking tray and the onion and peppers on another. Put both trays into the oven and bake for about 25 minutes, or until the sweet potatoes are soft. The onions and peppers are even better baked for about 5 minutes longer, to dry them out and intensify the flavours, but if it's easier, take them out together. Leave the oven turned on, as you will be using it later.

Put the sweet potatoes into a large bowl and add the chickpeas, garlic, lemon juice, cumin, coriander, paprika, cayenne, black pepper, salt and tamari. Either blitz the mix together, using a stick blender or food processor, or simply mash with a potato masher. Make sure everything is mixed thoroughly and that there are no big lumps left.

Finely chop the scallions or spring onions, red onion and fresh herbs and add to the mixture along with the cumin seeds. These will add texture and colour as well as flavour. Mix well.

Divide the mixture into four and form each portion into a large burger-shaped cake or patty. Sprinkle the sesame seeds on a plate, then turn the cakes over in the

seeds until they are coated on both sides. Place the patties on a baking tray and bake for 15–20 minutes – to get them extra crisp, flip them over halfway through.

Put the baked red peppers and onion into a medium pan on a high heat along with the tinned tomatoes and the rest of the relish ingredients. Once the mixture starts to boil, reduce the heat and simmer for 10 minutes. Blend the mixture together and your relish is ready to serve.

Serve the falafel cakes with the relish on top. They also go great with hummus, toasted pitta breads and a fresh green salad.

# VIETNAMESE COCONUT CURRY SERVES 4

A deliciously simple pumpkin and coconut curry using tempeh (see page 231). This recipe is low-fat and always a favourite on our Happy Heart course.

3 cloves of garlic • a thumb-size piece of fresh ginger • 1 medium pumpkin (approx. 1.5kg) (if not available, use butternut squash or sweet potatoes) • 2 x 400ml tins of low-fat coconut milk • juice of 2 limes • 2 tablespoons honey • 2 tablespoons curry powder • 1 teaspoon salt • 4 tablespoons tamari, Bragg Liquid Aminos or soy sauce • 1 x 300g pack of tempeh (if not available, use firm tofu) • ½ a head of pak choi • 6 scallions or 4 spring onions • a decent bunch of fresh coriander • 1 tablespoon cornflour, arrowroot or potato starch, mixed with 1½ tablespoons water

Preheat the oven to 200°C/400°F/gas mark 6.

Peel and finely chop the garlic. Peel and finely grate or chop the ginger.

Wash the pumpkin, cut off any blemishes and slice off the top. Usually there is no need to peel it, as the skin goes soft when cooked. Cut it in half and scoop out the seeds. Cut the flesh into bite-size pieces. (If using butternut squash or sweet potatoes, leave the skin on and cut into bite-size pieces.) Put on a baking tray and bake for 20 minutes.

Put the garlic, ginger, coconut milk, lime juice, honey, curry powder, salt and tamari into a blender and whiz until everything is smooth.

Cut the tempeh into small cubes (around 1.5cm). Put into an oven dish, pour over half the coconut dressing and mix well – this ensures each piece is full of flavour.

Put the dish of tempeh into the oven where the pumpkin is already baking and bake for 15 minutes, stirring after 10 minutes to ensure that the dressing is well dispersed. Meanwhile, pour the other half of the dressing into a large pan – this will become the sauce, along with any remaining sauce from the baked tempeh dish. Bring to the boil, then lower the heat and reduce to a simmer.

Once the tempeh and pumpkin are done, transfer them to the simmering sauce and mix well. Cook for 10 minutes over a medium heat, stirring regularly.

Now finely chop the pak choi, scallions or spring onions and coriander. Add the pak choi and the cornflour mixture to the pan and simmer for about 3–5 minutes, until it thickens. Serve sprinkled with the scallions or spring onions and the coriander.

Great with wholewheat noodles, brown rice or wholemeal couscous.

# VERONICA'S GREEN BEAN CURRY SERVES 4

This is Dave's mother-in-law's simple green bean curry. We nearly always eat this as a side dish, alongside the potato and bean curry on the next page. Using fresh green beans in this dish will cost you three times as much as frozen, and they will take a bit longer to cook, as they are more fibrous. Frozen beans cook more quickly and are cheaper!

750g frozen green beans • 1 onion • 1 tomato • 5 cloves of garlic • 3 tablespoons oil • 1 tablespoon black mustard seeds (optional) • 1 teaspoon ground turmeric • 2½ teaspoons curry powder • 1½ teaspoons salt

Take the beans out of the freezer and leave them to thaw gently at room temperature while you prepare the other ingredients. Peel and finely chop the onion. Chop the tomato. Peel and crush the garlic.

Put the oil into a wide-bottomed pan over a high heat. When it's hot, reduce the heat to medium and add the onion and tomato. Put the lid on and cook for 5 minutes, stirring every now and then. Stir in the garlic and mustard seeds (if using) and continue to cook for another 5 minutes with the lid on, stirring occasionally. Add the turmeric and curry powder and stir well. Cook for a further 2 minutes, stirring frequently.

Add the beans (they will be thawed enough by now) and the salt and stir well so that they get an even coating of onion and tomato. Add a couple of tablespoons of water and leave to simmer, covered, on a low heat for 20 minutes (if you can leave it for 45 minutes over a very low heat, it comes together even better).

Tip: If it is the right time of the year for bergamot lemons, a squeeze of the juice over the finished dish really sets these beans apart from the crowd!

# VERONICA'S POTATO AND BEAN CURRY SERVES 4

This is Dave's mother-in-law, Veronica's, recipe. She is Indian, so this is the real deal. It is simple, yet elegant and very satisfying. You can cook it in 25 minutes if necessary, but if you have the time to cook it slowly the flavours really infuse, the sauce thickens and it's even nicer!

- 1 medium onion
- 1 medium tomato
- 3 cloves of garlic
- 2cm cube of fresh ginger
- 4 tablespoons oil
- 3 large potatoes
- 1 teaspoon ground turmeric
- 1½ tablespoons medium curry powder
- 2 x 400g tins of kidney beans (or any other kind of bean)
- 2 teaspoons salt
- a small bunch of fresh coriander
- freshly ground black pepper

Peel and finely chop the onion and finely dice the tomato. Peel the garlic and ginger, then crush them together in a pestle and mortar.

Put the oil into a family-size wide-bottomed pan over a high heat and leave for 3 minutes. When the oil is hot, turn the heat down and add the onions and tomatoes, leaving them to simmer for 5 minutes with the lid on, stirring occasionally. Add the garlic and ginger and continue to simmer for a further 5–7 minutes, covered, still stirring from time to time. Meanwhile cut the potatoes lengthways into medium wedges and put the kettle on to boil.

Add the turmeric and curry powder to the pan of onions and tomatoes and stir well. Simmer for 3 minutes, still on a low to medium heat, stirring frequently. Add a tablespoon of water if anything starts to stick.

Drain the beans and rinse them thoroughly. Add the beans, potatoes and salt along with 300ml of boiling water and stir well so that the potatoes and beans are well coated in the sauce. Turn the heat up and bring to the boil, then reduce to a simmer for 30–40 minutes. Stir every 10 minutes or so, so that the potatoes cook evenly. (Depending on the type of potatoes, the dish might be cooked and good to serve in 25–30 minutes – however, if you have the time, leaving it to simmer for an extra 15 minutes will make it taste even better!)

Finely chop the coriander and add to the pan a few minutes before serving. Taste and add more salt and some freshly ground black pepper if needed.

# AUBERGINE, FENNEL AND BEAN STEW SERVES 4–6

This has lovely hints of aniseed from the fennel, musky undertones of cumin and the subtle aromas of cardamom. It tastes even better the next day!

2 medium onions • 3 cloves of garlic • ½ a thumb-size piece of fresh ginger • 1 fresh green chilli • 1½ aubergines • 700g pumpkin • 2 tablespoons cumin seeds • 1 tablespoon fennel seeds • 2 tablespoons oil • 3 tablespoons tamari, Bragg Liquid Aminos or soy sauce • 1 teaspoon paprika • 3 teaspoons salt • 1 x 400g tin of black beans • 2 teaspoons ground cardamom • 1 tablespoon ground turmeric • 2 x 400g tins of chopped tomatoes • 1 tablespoon honey or agave syrup • a small bunch of fresh coriander • 100g baby spinach

Peel the onions, garlic and ginger, then finely chop the onions, and crush or chop the garlic and ginger. Deseed and finely chop the chilli. Cut the aubergines and pumpkin into bite-size pieces, leaving the skin on the pumpkin.

Put the cumin and fennel seeds into a dry frying pan and cook on a medium heat for a few minutes, until they start to release their aroma and start crackling. Transfer the seeds to a pestle and mortar or coffee grinder and grind them to a fine powder.

Put the oil into a large pan over a high heat and let it heat up for about 2 minutes. Once it is hot, add the onions and turn the heat to low to medium. Sauté the onions for 5 minutes with the lid on, stirring regularly. Add the garlic, chilli, ginger and the ground cumin and fennel and cook, covered, for a further 5 minutes, stirring regularly.

Add the aubergines, along with the tamari and paprika. Leave to cook, covered, for 10–15 minutes on a low to medium heat, stirring regularly. Add water a tablespoon at a time if anything starts to stick to the bottom of the pan. After a few minutes the aubergines should start to break up.

Put the pumpkin into a separate pan with 1 teaspoon of salt and enough water to cover. Bring to the boil, then reduce to a simmer for about 15–20 minutes, until the pumpkin is tender. Drain and set aside.

Drain the beans and rinse thoroughly. Stir the cardamom, turmeric and 2 table-spoons of water into the pan of aubergines and cook for 1 minute. Add the beans, tinned tomatoes, honey, pumpkin and the remaining 2 teaspoons of salt and turn the heat up high. Bring to the boil, then reduce to a gentle simmer for 15 minutes.

Five minutes before serving, finely chop the coriander and add to the pan with the spinach. Great served with brown rice or flatbreads if you have time to make them (see page 41).

# MEXICAN LEEK AND BLACK BEAN CHILLI SERVES 4

A really quick dinner – great served with brown rice, baked potatoes or some toasted wholemeal pitta breads cut into soldiers and accompanied by crème fraîche or sour cream.

- 1 red onion
- 4 cloves of garlic
- 1 red pepper
- 1 yellow pepper
- ½ teaspoon ground chilli or 1 whole fresh chilli
- 2 medium leeks
- 2 tablespoons oil
- 1 teaspoon cumin seed
- 2 teaspoons salt
- 1 x 400g tins of black beans
- 2 x 400g tins of chopped tomatoes
- 100g tomato purée
- 1 teaspoon ground coriander
- 1 teaspoon ground cumin
- ¼ teaspoon smoked paprika
- ¼ teaspoon freshly ground black pepper
- 1 tablespoon honey
- 20g fresh coriander
- juice of ½ a lime

Peel and finely chop the onion and garlic. Deseed the peppers, and the fresh chilli if using, and slice them with the leeks (including the green parts).

Heat the oil in a big pan and fry the onion and garlic on a medium heat for 5 minutes, stirring regularly to ensure they don't get burnt. Add the sliced leeks and peppers along with the chilli, cumin seed and salt, and fry for a further 5 minutes.

Drain the black beans and rinse thoroughly. Add to the pan with the tinned tomatoes, tomato purée, ground coriander, ground cumin, paprika, black pepper and honey. Turn the heat to high and bring to the boil, then reduce the heat and leave to simmer for a further 10 minutes.

Finely chop the fresh coriander and stir through with the lime juice. Taste, and season with more salt and pepper if needed. Enjoy!

# INDONESIAN AUBERGINE SATAY  SERVES 4

This is a lovely rich, creamy and peanutty dish, with the addition of roasted aubergines and the meaty tempeh.

- 3 aubergines
- 2 carrots
- 200g green beans
- 2 onions
- 0.5cm piece of fresh ginger
- 3 cloves of garlic
- 1 fresh red chilli
- 4 tablespoons tamari, Bragg Liquid Aminos or soy sauce
- 100ml orange juice
- 1 teaspoon ground ginger
- 300g tempeh or tofu, cut into small pieces
- 5 tablespoons oil
- salt and freshly ground black pepper
- 4 tablespoons smooth peanut butter
- 2 tablespoons apple cider vinegar
- 2 tablespoons honey
- ½ a head of pak choi
- a bunch of fresh coriander
- 100g beansprouts
- toasted nuts to garnish (optional)

Preheat the oven to 200°C/400°F/gas mark 6.

Cut the aubergines into bite-size pieces and the carrots into bite-size rounds. Trim the green beans and cut them in half. Peel and finely slice the onions, ginger and garlic. Deseed and finely slice the chilli.

Put the tamari, orange juice and ground ginger into a meduim bowl and mix together. Cut the tempeh into small pieces and add to the mix, then stir to coat evenly. Put the tempeh with its marinade on a baking tray and bake for 25 minutes.

Put the aubergines into a separate bowl and pour over 3 tablespoons of the oil. Add a couple of pinches of salt and mix well, then spread the aubergines out on a baking tray and roast in the oven for 30 minutes.

Bring a small pan of water to the boil. Add the carrots and cook for 5 minutes, then add the green beans and cook for a further 1 minute. Drain and cool under cold running water. You want them still to have a bit of bite, as they will cook more later on. Leave to one side.

Put the remaining 2 tablespoons of oil into a wide-bottomed pan. When the oil is hot, reduce the heat, add the onion and sauté for 5 minutes, stirring occasionally. Add the garlic, ginger and chilli and cook for 3 minutes, stirring regularly. If the mix is becoming too dry, add a few spoonfuls of warm water.

In a bowl or jug, whisk together the peanut butter, apple cider vinegar, honey and 350ml of warm water until smooth. Add this to the pan along with the baked tempeh and aubergines, and mix through.

Bring to the boil on a high heat, then reduce the heat and simmer for 10 minutes. If the sauce becomes too thick, add a little more water.

SOY

Taste and season with salt and pepper. Cut the pak choi into bite-size pieces and add to the pan, along with the carrots and greens beans, 5 minutes before serving.

Chop the coriander, rinse the beansprouts, and sprinkle over each serving. If you have any toasted nuts, these go great as a garnish too. Serve with brown basmati rice.

# PUY LENTIL COCONUT DAHL · SERVES 4–6

This dahl is super-comforting and hearty. The coconut milk adds depth to the flavour, and the pumpkin, cherry tomatoes and pak choi give it plenty of colour.

3 cloves of garlic • 1 small green (kabocha) or orange pumpkin (about 450g) (see page 225), or 1 butternut squash • 3 medium potatoes • 1 medium leek • 400g Puy lentils, or other green or brown lentils • 2 tablespoons oil • 1 x 400ml tin of coconut milk (use low-fat if concerned about calories) • 1 x 400g tin of chopped tomatoes • 2½ teaspoons salt • 6 tablespoons tamari, Bragg Liquid Aminos or soy sauce • juice of 1 lemon • 1 head of pak choi • 150g cherry tomatoes or 2 regular tomatoes
**For the spice mix** • 2½ tablespoons ground coriander (use whole seeds if you have them) • 2½ tablespoons ground cumin (use whole seeds if you have them) • ½ teaspoon freshly ground black pepper • 2 teaspoons ground turmeric • 2 teaspoons ground ginger • 1 teaspoon ground cinnamon • 3 teaspoons medium curry powder • 1 teaspoon paprika • a pinch of chilli powder or cayenne pepper

If using whole coriander and cumin seeds, grind them into a fine powder in a pestle and mortar or in a coffee grinder. Mix all the spices in a small dish.

Peel and finely chop the garlic. Cut the unpeeled potatoes and pumpkin into bite-size pieces (if using a butternut squash, peel it first). Finely chop the leek. Put the lentils into a colander and rinse under cold running water.

Put the oil into a large family-size pan over a medium heat and warm for 2 minutes. Lower the heat to low to medium, add the garlic and leek and sauté for 5 minutes with the lid on, stirring regularly. Add the spice mix and sauté for a further 3 minutes, stirring continuously. If the spices are sticking to the base of the pan, add a couple of tablespoons of water and keep stirring.

Add the pumpkin, potatoes, coconut milk, tinned tomatoes, salt, tamari, lemon juice and lentils to the pan, pour in 1 litre of water, and turn up the heat. Bring to the boil, then reduce to a simmer for about 30 minutes, or until the lentils are cooked (they should feel soft and break up between your fingers). Stir regularly, adding more water if the dahl is becoming too thick.

Slice the pak choi into bite-size strips and halve the cherry tomatoes, or chop regular ones. Stir them into the dish 2 minutes before serving and heat through. Season with more salt and pepper if needed.

The final consistency of the dahl should be reasonably dry, while still having enough liquid – something like a stew.

SOY

# DAVE'S THAI RED CURRY SERVES 4-6

Dave likes making curries! This is his take on a Thai red curry. He always adds a bit of beetroot to give it a red/pink colour and a little sweetness.

500g firm tofu or tempeh • 4 tablespoons tamari, Bragg Liquid Aminos or soy sauce • juice of 3 limes • 3 shallots or 1 medium onion • 3 cloves of garlic • 1 thumb-size piece of fresh ginger • 3 stalks of lemongrass • 3 fresh red chillies • 1 red pepper • 100g uncooked beetroot • 1 courgette • 1 head of broccoli • 1 large sweet potato • 6 scallions or 4 spring onions • 2 tablespoons oil • 2 teaspoons salt • 2 x 400ml tins of coconut milk • 2 teaspoons ground cumin • 2 teaspoons ground coriander • 4 kaffir lime leaves (or the zest of a lime) • ½ teaspoon freshly ground black pepper • 1 tablespoon agave syrup or honey • 15g fresh basil, leaves picked (optional)

Cut the tofu or tempeh into small cubes (the smaller you dice it the more surface area there is to marinate and enhance the flavour). Put it into a bowl and add the tamari and lime juice. Mix thoroughly so that each piece gets an even coating and leave to marinate.

Peel and finely chop the shallots, garlic and ginger. Crush the lemongrass with the back of a knife. Deseed the chillies and red pepper, then finely chop the chillies and cut the pepper into bite-size pieces. Scrub the beetroot and grate it into a bowl. Cut the courgette into bite-size pieces and the broccoli into small florets. Cut the sweet potato into bite-size pieces. Finely slice the scallions or spring onions.

Put the oil into a large family-size pan over a high heat. Let it heat up for 2 minutes, then reduce to a low to medium heat and add the shallots, garlic, ginger, lemongrass and chillies. Cook for 7 minutes, stirring regularly.

Remove the tofu or tempeh from its marinade with a slotted spoon (keeping the marinade) and add along with the beetroot and salt. Continue cooking for 5 minutes, stirring regularly. Add the coconut milk, cumin, coriander, kaffir lime leaves, black pepper and agave syrup and stir well, then cook for 3 minutes. Add the courgette, sweet potato, red pepper and the tofu/tempeh together with its marinade. Cook for 15-20 minutes.

Add the broccoli and scallions or spring onions 5 minutes before the end. Remove the basil leaves from the stalks, if using, and add as a garnish just before serving.

Serve with brown basmati rice or Thai rice noodles.

# INDIAN VEG KORMA SERVES 4–6

This is a lovely simple coconut korma with a rich well-seasoned sauce. This dish is not spicy, and is hearty, with its potatoes and pea combo. It's good with brown basmati rice or short-grain brown rice, and is also great served with toasted pitta breads drizzled with a little oil and a pinch of salt and cut up into little soldiers!

1 onion • 3 decent-size cloves of garlic • 1.5cm cube of fresh ginger • 1 fresh chilli • 1 medium tomato • 1 courgette • 1 leek • 750g potatoes • 100g green beans or mangetout • 250g frozen peas • 2 tablespoons oil • 1 x 400ml tin of coconut milk • 3 tablespoons tamari, Bragg Liquid Aminos or soy sauce • juice of 1 lemon • 1 tablespoon agave syrup or honey • 2 teaspoons ground cumin • 2 teaspoons ground coriander • 1 teaspoon ground turmeric • 4 teaspoons medium curry powder • 2 teaspoons salt • ½ teaspoon freshly ground black pepper • 1 x 400g tin of chickpeas • a small bunch of fresh coriander

Peel and finely chop the onion, garlic and ginger. Deseed and finely chop the chilli (keep the seeds in if you like it hot). Finely dice the tomato. Cut the courgette, leek and potatoes into bite-size pieces. Trim the green beans and cut them in half. Put the frozen peas into a bowl of warm water.

Heat the oil in a large family-size pan over a high heat for 2 minutes, then reduce the heat to low and add the onion and tomato. Stir regularly, keeping the lid on, and cook gently for 10 minutes. Check regularly, adding a little water if the onions start to stick to the bottom of the pan.

Add the garlic, ginger and chilli, and continue cooking for a further 5 minutes. Add the coconut milk, tamari, lemon juice, agave syrup, cumin, coriander, turmeric, curry powder, salt and black pepper and cook for another 3 minutes, stirring regularly.

Drain and rinse the chickpeas and add to the pan with the courgette, leek and potatoes. Turn the heat up high, bring to the boil, then reduce the heat and leave to simmer over a low heat for about 15 minutes.

Drain the peas and add with the green beans, then simmer for 5 minutes. Check that the potatoes are properly cooked before serving.

Finely chop the fresh coriander, stalks and all, and add just before serving.

SOY

# SRI LANKAN VEG CURRY SERVES 4

This is a fantastic recipe. It's one of Phil's, and it looks amazing – really vibrant and colourful. It is very straightforward to make and has a lovely full flavour.

2 tablespoons cumin seeds • 2½ tablespoons coriander seeds • 2 tablespoons fennel seeds • 1 tablespoon black peppercorns • 1 red pepper • 1 yellow pepper • ½ a green chilli • 2 aubergines • 4 carrots • ½ a small head of broccoli • 1 onion • a thumb-size piece of fresh ginger • 4 tablespoons sunflower oil • 2 teaspoons salt • 1 teaspoon ground turmeric • 1 teaspoon ground ginger • 1 x 400g tin of chopped tomatoes • 1 x 400ml tin of coconut milk • juice of ½ a lemon • 2 tablespoons agave syrup or honey • 100g baby spinach • a small bunch of fresh coriander

Preheat the oven to 200°C/400°F/gas mark 6.

Toast the cumin, coriander and fennel seeds in a dry pan on a medium heat. When they start to pop, turn golden and release their aromas, turn the heat off and let them cool down. Grind the spices and peppercorns to a fine powder in a pestle and mortar or a coffee grinder. (Use ground spices if you don't have whole.)

Deseed the peppers and chilli, then cut the peppers into bite-size pieces and finely chop the chilli. Cut the aubergines and carrots into bite-size pieces. Break the broccoli into small florets. Peel and finely chop the onion and peel and grate the ginger.

Put the aubergines into a bowl with 2 tablespoons of the oil and ½ teaspoon of salt, stir to coat evenly, then put on a baking tray. Put the peppers and carrots on a separate tray. Put both trays into the oven and roast the vegetables for 25–30 minutes. If you think of it, give them a mix after 15 minutes to ensure they cook evenly.

Bring a pan of water to the boil and blanch the broccoli florets for 30 seconds, then drain and cool under running cold water.

Put the remaining 2 tablespoons of oil into a wide-bottomed pan on a low to medium heat. Add the onion and fry for about 8 minutes until it softens, stirring regularly. Add the fresh ginger, chilli, turmeric, ground ginger and the toasted spices and cook for a further 3 minutes, stirring constantly. If anything starts to stick to the bottom of the pan, add a little water.

Add the tinned tomatoes, coconut milk, lemon juice, agave syrup and the remaining 1½ teaspoons of salt and turn the heat up to medium. When it boils, reduce the heat to low again and simmer for 20 minutes, or until the sauce begins to thicken slightly. Add the roasted vegetables, broccoli and spinach and mix well with the sauce.

Chop the coriander finely (stalks and all) and add to the dish before serving.

# VIETNAMESE SWEET ALMOND CURRY SERVES 6

Vietnamese food is among the healthiest in the world, full of fresh veg, spices and herbs. This curry goes well with short-grain brown rice.

1 medium butternut squash • 2 red peppers • 1 fresh red chilli • 1 aubergine • 1 leek • 3 cloves of garlic • 1cm cube of fresh ginger • 2 stalks of lemongrass • 4 tablespoons oil • 6 tablespoons tamari, Bragg Liquid Aminos or soy sauce • 4 tablespoons almond butter • 1 x 400ml tin of coconut milk • juice of 2 limes • 2 tablespoons agave syrup or honey • 2 teaspoons ground turmeric • 2 teaspoons paprika • 2 teaspoons ground coriander • 1 tablespoon ground cumin • 2 teaspoons salt • ½ teaspoon freshly ground black pepper • 1 x 400g tin of black beans • 6 scallions or 4 spring onions • 1 x 227g pack of beansprouts • flaked almonds (optional)

Peel and deseed the butternut squash and cut it into bite-size pieces. Deseed the red peppers and the chilli, then cut the pepper into strips and finely slice the chilli (include the seeds if you like it hot). Cut the aubergine into bite-size pieces and slice the leek. Peel and finely chop the garlic and ginger. Crush the lemongrass.

Preheat the oven to 200°C/400°F/gas mark 6.

Put the squash, aubergine and peppers into a mixing bowl. Add 2 tablespoons of the oil together with 2 tablespoons of tamari and mix well. Transfer the mixed vegetables on to a baking tray and spread out evenly. Roast in the oven for 25 minutes.

Put the remaining oil into a large pan over a low to medium heat and let it heat up for 2 minutes. Add the leek, garlic, chilli, ginger and lemongrass and cook gently over a low heat for 10 minutes with the lid on, stirring occasionally.

Mix the almond butter with 500ml of water in a blender, or whisk with a fork in a bowl until smooth. Add to the pan along with the coconut milk, lime juice, agave syrup, turmeric, paprika, coriander, cumin, salt, black pepper and the remaining tamari and mix well. Bring to the boil, then reduce to a simmer for 10 minutes.

In the meantime, drain and rinse the black beans, slice the scallions or spring onions into small rounds and rinse the beansprouts. Add the black beans to the pan along with the roasted squash, peppers and aubergine and cook for a further 3 minutes.

Add the scallions or spring onions and beansprouts just before serving and, if you fancy, sprinkle some flaked almonds on top. (Don't add the beansprouts too early, otherwise they go soft and limp, and lose their crunch very quickly in heat.)

SOY

# SAMPHIRE, CIDER AND VEG CHOWDER SERVES 4–6

This is Claire's take on seafood chowder, the seafood being samphire. Samphire grows on riverbanks, in marshes and where the sea goes out. It has a unique salty taste and a vivid green colour.

- 3 shallots or 1 medium onion
- 200g swede (a.k.a. turnip in Ireland!)
- ½ a bulb of fennel
- 2 carrots
- 2 leeks
- 500g potatoes (preferably a slightly waxy potato that holds its shape when boiled)
- 1 x 400g tin of butter beans
- 750ml dry cider
- a bunch of fresh flat-leaf parsley
- a small bunch of fresh thyme
- 1 bay leaf
- 2 teaspoons salt
- 1.5 litres vegetable stock
- 1 x 400ml tin of coconut milk
- juice of ½ a lemon
- 200g fresh samphire
- freshly ground black pepper

**Optional funky additions**

5–10g dulse (dillisk) seaweed, added when boiling the potatoes

a few nettle leaves, added 15 minutes before the end

a handful of sea spinach (if you know what you are looking for), added with the fennel and leek

Peel and finely chop the shallots and swede. Cut the fennel, carrots, leeks and unpeeled potatoes into bite-size pieces. Drain the butter beans and rinse thoroughly.

Saute the shallots for 3 minutes over a medium heat. Add the cider, a bouquet garni (parsley, thyme and bay leaf tied together, see page 220), the swede, carrots, potatoes, salt (and the dulse, if you have some). Bring to the boil, then turn down to a simmer for 8–10 minutes.

Add the fennel and leeks to the pan along with the vegetable stock and simmer until the vegetables are tender and the stock has reduced down near the level of the vegetables (approx. 15 minutes). Add the coconut milk, butter beans and lemon juice and cook for a further 10 minutes on a low heat.

Bring a separate small pan of water to the boil. Add the samphire and blanch for 20–30 seconds, then drain and cool under cold running water. This gives the samphire a really vibrant green colour. Add to the pan just before serving, then taste and season with salt and pepper.

Great with fresh brown bread.

# BEETROOT, WALNUT AND FETA BURGERS WITH ROASTED CARROT HUMMUS AND SPROUTED SEED SALAD SERVES 4

A super-easy recipe. A lovely contrast of colours all topped off with a rockin' roasted carrot hummus! Created by Phil.

- 400g uncooked beetroot
- 6 scallions or 4 spring onions
- 80g vegetarian style Parmesan or mature Cheddar cheese
- 100g feta cheese
- 140g toasted walnuts
- 2 tablespoons oil
- 4 tablespoons finely chopped fresh mint
- 150g breadcrumbs
- juice of ½ a lemon
- roasted carrot hummus – see page 97

**For the salad topping**
- 10g alfalfa sprouts
- 20g toasted sunflower seeds
- 1 tablespoon finely chopped chives

If you are going to bake your burgers, preheat the oven to 200°C/400°F/gas mark 6.

Scrub and grate the beetroot. Finely chop the scallions or spring onions. Grate the Parmesan, crumble the feta and roughly chop the walnuts.

Put the oil into a medium pan on a medium heat and let it heat up for 2 minutes. Add the beetroot to the pan, along with the scallions or spring onions, and continue cooking for a few more minutes. Set aside to cool for a minute.

Put the beetroot mixture into a medium bowl with both the cheeses, the mint, walnuts, breadcrumbs and a squeeze of lemon. Mix well, using your hands. Taste and add salt and black pepper if it needs it. Form into burger-shaped patties. (If too dry, add some beaten egg; if too wet, add some flour.)

To bake your patties, put them on a baking tray lined with greaseproof paper and bake in the oven for 25 minutes, turning them over halfway through. Otherwise fry them in a little oil in a non-stick pan for 5 minutes on each side.

Mix together the ingredients for the salad topping. Top the cooked beetroot burgers generously with the carrot hummus, and serve with the sprout salad on the very top.

# QUINOA, BUTTERBEAN AND BUTTERNUT SQUASH BURGER  MAKES 4–5 BURGERS

These are really tasty and look great, a lovely golden colour. They keep well for a couple of days in the fridge and are good served with slices of ripe avocado.

200g quinoa • 380ml water • zest of 1 lemon • 2 teaspoons sumac (paprika is also fine if you don't have sumac) • leaves from 7 sprigs of fresh thyme • 1 red onion • 1 medium butternut squash • 1 x 400g tin of butter beans • 1 teaspoon salt • 3 teaspoons balsamic vinegar • 2 tablespoons chopped fresh parsley • 8 sun-dried tomatoes • 1 tablespoon toasted sesame seeds • 1 tablespoon lemon juice • 1 small clove of garlic • 2 tablespoons olive oil • ½ teaspoon salt

Preheat the oven to 200°C/400°F/gas mark 6.

Put the quinoa, water, lemon zest, sumac and thyme into a medium pan. Bring to the boil, then reduce to a simmer and cook, covered, until all the water is absorbed. Set aside.

Peel the red onion and slice into half-moons. Peel and halve the butternut squash, take the seeds out, and roughly chop the flesh. Drain the butter beans and rinse thoroughly.

Put the sliced onions into a bowl and add 2 teaspoons of balsamic vinegar. Transfer them to one end of a lined baking tray, with the butternut squash at the other (or use 2 baking trays). Roast in the oven for 30 minutes. Leave the oven on, as you will need it later.

Put half the quinoa mixture into a large bowl and add half the butter beans, the roasted red onions and the parsley. Mix well together. Put the other half of the quinoa and butter beans into a food processor and add the sun-dried tomatoes, roasted squash, sesame seeds, lemon juice, peeled garlic, olive oil, salt and the remaining teaspoon of balsamic vinegar. Blend until smooth. (If you don't have a food processor, simply chop the sun-dried tomatoes and garlic and use a potato masher to mash it all together.)

Add the blended mixture to the bowl of quinoa and mix well. Shape into burger-shaped patties, using your hands. At this stage the mixture should feel wet, but it will solidify once baked. Put the burgers on a baking tray lined with baking parchment and roast in the oven for 35 minutes.

Serve topped with slices of ripe avocado, and with hummus or harissa alongside.

# PUY LENTIL AND CORIANDER PESTO BAKE WITH SWEET POTATO MASH SERVES 6–8

A simple bake that tastes even better on day two! The coriander pesto sets the lentils alight, and it looks really well if you keep back a little to drizzle on top before serving. Serve with a simple green salad.

2 medium carrots • 150g green beans • 250g potatoes • 750g sweet potatoes • 400g Puy lentils, or other green or brown lentils • 2 bay leaves • leaves from 6 sprigs of fresh thyme • 2 teaspoons salt • 1 teaspoon freshly ground black pepper • 50ml tamari • approx. 100ml non-dairy milk • approx. 1 teaspoon salt • a pinch of freshly ground black pepper
**For the pesto** • a good bunch of fresh coriander (approx.50g) • 3 cloves of garlic • 1 teaspoon salt • 100ml oil • 100ml water

Cut the carrots into bite-size pieces. Trim the green beans and cut them in half. Cut the unpeeled potatoes and sweet potatoes into evenly sized pieces.

Rinse the lentils and put them into a large family-size pan with the carrots, bay leaves, thyme, salt, black pepper, tamari and 1 litre of water. Turn the heat up high and put the lid on the pan. Bring to the boil, then reduce the heat, leave the lid ajar so that the steam can evaporate, and simmer for a further 25 minutes, until the lentils are cooked and nearly all the liquid has gone.

Put the potatoes and sweet potatoes into a large pan with enough water to cover. Bring to the boil, then reduce the heat and simmer for about 15 minutes, until tender. Drain, then put them back into the pan and mash with a potato masher or fork, slowly adding the milk and mashing as you go until you reach the desired consistency. Season with salt and black pepper.

Preheat the oven to 200°C/400°F/gas mark 6.

Roughly chop the coriander (leaves and stalks) and put into a blender or food processor with the peeled whole cloves of garlic and the other pesto ingredients. Blend until reasonably smooth.

Once the lentils are soft and cooked through, stir in the coriander pesto and add the green beans.

Put the lentil mix into a baking dish and cover with the mash, spiking it up with your fork so that you get some crispy bits. Bake in the oven for 25 minutes.

# WINTER SQUASH, LEEK, KALE AND FENNEL GRATIN SERVES 4–6

One of Phil's super-wholesome and hearty bakes. The colours of the kale, squash and fennel look great together. This is a hearty one to savour with a nice glass of wine!

2 bulbs of fennel • 1 medium winter squash • 2 leeks • 2 cloves of garlic • 150g kale • 3 tablespoons olive oil • 3 teaspoons salt • 100g hazelnuts • 10 sprigs of fresh thyme • 125ml cream • 1 teaspoon Dijon mustard • a squeeze of lemon juice • 100g feta cheese • 50g breadcrumbs • 25g Cheddar cheese, grated

Halve the fennel bulbs and slice each one into 5 or 6 pieces lengthways. Peel the squash and cut into chunky pieces. Cut the leeks into bite-size pieces. Peel and mince the garlic. Remove the kale stalks and cut the leaves into pieces.

Preheat the oven to 200°C/400°F/gas mark 6.

Bring a pan of water to the boil. Add the fennel and cook for 8–10 minutes, until soft. Drain, then put on a baking tray lined with greaseproof paper. Put the squash on another baking tray and drizzle each tray with a tablespoon of olive oil. Sprinkle with salt and roast in the oven for 30 minutes. Once cooked, remove from the oven but don't turn it off.

Put the hazelnuts (no need to skin) into a dry pan on a medium heat for 8–10 minutes. Let them cool, then blitz them roughly in a food processor.

Put 1 tablespoon of oil into a separate pan on a medium heat and add the leeks and a teaspoon of salt. After 5 minutes add the garlic, thyme leaves and another teaspoon of salt and sauté for a further 5 minutes. Add the cream and mustard, then turn the heat to low and continue cooking for another 5 minutes. Add the roasted squash and break up the chunky pieces with a fork.

Put the kale leaves into a mixing bowl and add 1 tablespoon of oil, a pinch of salt and a squeeze of lemon juice. Massage the leaves with your hands until the colour changes to a darker green and the leaves soften. Add the feta and hazelnuts and mix well.

Spread the leek and squash mix in a baking dish, followed by the kale mix. Put the fennel on top, and finally top with the breadcrumbs and Cheddar. Roast in the oven for about 25 minutes.

# TASTY VEG BAKE IN A ROASTED RED PEPPER AND ALMOND CREAM SAUCE SERVES 6–8

You can make this dish throughout the year using whatever veg are in season, so don't feel restricted. It is the sauce that really stands out in this dish. It is mixed right through the bake, making it very rich and luxurious.

**For the sauce**
- 3 red peppers
- 200ml cream
- 100g almond butter
- 1½ teaspoons salt
- ½ teaspoon freshly ground black pepper

**For the veg mix**
- 300g celeriac
- 1 medium squash
- 1 head of cauliflower
- 2 leeks
- 4 scallions or 2 spring onions
- 2 cloves of garlic
- 250g baby spinach
- 2 tablespoons oil
- 120g feta cheese
- a large bunch of fresh basil

**For the topping**
- a handful of flaked almonds
- a handful of pumpkin seeds
- 1 good handful of grated Cheddar cheese

Preheat the oven to 200°C/400°F/gas mark 6.

Put the whole red peppers on a baking tray. Peel the celeriac and squash and cut them into bite-size pieces. Put them on a second baking tray, and put both trays into the oven for 35–40 minutes. The peppers are ready when the skins are blistered. Remove from the oven, but don't turn it off.

In the meantime, cut the cauliflower into florets. Thinly slice the leeks and scallions or spring onions. Peel and finely slice the garlic.

Cook the cauliflower in a steamer for 3–5 minutes. Once tender, put it into a large bowl. Steam the spinach for 1 minute and add to the bowl. Heat the oil in a medium pan and sauté the leeks, scallions or spring onions and garlic for 8 minutes over a medium heat, or until they become soft. Add to the bowl.

Once the peppers have cooled down, remove the stalks and seeds, then blend with the cream, almond butter, salt, pepper and 100ml of water.

Put all the vegetables into an ovenproof baking dish with the red pepper sauce, the feta and the basil leaves. Mix the almond flakes, pumpkin seeds and Cheddar in a small bowl and sprinkle on top of the dish. Bake in the oven for 30–40 minutes.

# GREEK PUMPKIN, FETA AND FILO PIE
## MAKES 6 LARGE OR 8 SMALL PORTIONS

One of Dave's twists on a spanakopita. It has lots of lovely fresh veg and the added taste sensation of the feta, all topped with crispy filo pastry ... what's not to love! This dish is easy to make and you can prepare it ahead of time and keep it in the fridge until you're ready to bake it.

250g frozen filo pastry • 500g pumpkin or butternut squash • 1 head of broccoli • 1 leek • 1 red onion • 6 cloves of garlic • 30g fresh mint • 30g fresh dill • 30g fresh curly or flat-leaf parsley • 250g fresh spinach • 300g feta cheese • 100g Cheddar cheese • 5 medium eggs • 1–1½ teaspoons salt (depending on how salty the feta is) • ½ teaspoon freshly ground black pepper • 1½ teaspoons ground cinnamon • 1 teaspoon nutmeg • 4 teaspoons dried mixed herbs • juice of ½ a lemon • olive oil, for brushing • 2 tablespoons sesame seeds or nigella seeds

Take the filo pastry out of the freezer 2 hours before you want to use it.

Deseed the unpeeled pumpkin or peeled squash and cut into bite-size pieces. Cut the broccoli into florets. Cut the leek into bite-size pieces. Peel and finely slice the red onion. Peel and finely slice the garlic. Chop the herbs (use just the leaves of the mint, but the leaves and stalks of the dill and parsley).

Put the pumpkin into a pan and cover with cold salted water. Bring to the boil, then cook for 15–20 minutes, until tender. Once cooked, remove with a slotted spoon and set aside. Leave the water simmering away.

Add the leeks and broccoli to the pan of water and blanch for about 4 minutes. Remove with a slotted spoon and cool under cold running water. Leave the water simmering away. Plunge the spinach into the same pan for 30 seconds to 1 minute, then remove with a slotted spoon, cool under running water, and set aside.

Put all the blanched vegetables into a colander and leave them in the sink for a few minutes to drain. Then transfer them to a large bowl, crumble in the feta and grate in the Cheddar. Add the red onion, garlic and fresh herbs and mix thoroughly (it should be quite dry and have lots of lovely colours, with the feta well mixed through it).

Preheat the oven to 200°C/400°F/gas mark 6.

Break the eggs into a separate mixing bowl. Add the salt, black pepper, cinnamon, nutmeg, dried herbs and lemon juice and mix it all together using a whisk or a fork. Add the egg mix to the vegetables and stir until well combined.

Now put the veg mix into a large family-size ovenproof casserole dish.

Put 1 layer of filo pastry on top of the veg mix and use a pastry brush to brush the top of the sheet very lightly with olive oil. Put another sheet of filo pastry on top (slightly rumple each sheet to leave a pocket for air, as it bakes crispier this way). Repeat this process till you have 4–5 sheets of filo on top of the dish. Give the top layer a generous brush of olive oil.

Sprinkle over the sesame or nigella seeds and bake in the oven for 35 minutes or until the filo is golden and crispy (if you are cooking it straight from the fridge it may take a few minutes longer).

# HAPPY PEAR WHITE LASAGNE SERVES 6

A mixture of one of Steve's and one of Dorene's dishes. A lovely spring lasagne that feels lighter and fresher than the typical tomato-based version. The béchamel and fresh herbs make this dish.

2 courgettes • 1 large squash or winter pumpkin • 1½ teaspoons salt • 1 big head of broccoli • 100g baby spinach • 150g feta cheese • 200g lasagne sheets • 75g Cheddar cheese
**For the béchamel sauce** • 1 small onion • 2 cloves of garlic • 1.25 litres milk • 3 sprigs of fresh parsley • ½ teaspoon grated nutmeg • 6 peppercorns • 1 bay leaf • leaves from 1 good bunch of mint • leaves from 1 good bunch of basil • 100g butter or 100ml oil • 100g plain white or spelt flour • 1½ teaspoons salt • ½ teaspoon freshly ground black pepper • zest of 1 small lemon • juice of ½ a small lemon • 100g strong-flavoured hard cheese, e.g. vegetarian style Parmesan or mature Cheddar

Preheat the oven to 180°C/350°F/gas mark 4.

Cut the courgettes and the squash (peeled) or pumpkin (unpeeled) into bite-size pieces. Spread evenly on a baking tray, sprinkle with 1 teaspoon of the salt, and bake in the oven for 25 minutes. When the veg are cooked, take them out of the oven, but don't turn it off.

Meanwhile, cut the broccoli into small florets and steam for 5 minutes (if you don't have a steamer, cook in boiling water for 3 minutes, then blanch in cold water to stop the broccoli cooking and retain its vibrant green colour).

Peel and finely chop the onion and garlic. Put into a medium pan with the milk, parsley, nutmeg, peppercorns and bay leaf and bring to a gentle boil on a medium heat, stirring occasionally to prevent burning. Once the milk begins to bubble, turn the heat off and leave to infuse for 15 minutes.

Finely chop the mint and basil. Melt the butter or heat the oil gently over a low heat. Whisk the flour into the fat for about 5 minutes, until the flour is absorbed. You will be left with a thick paste (a roux). Strain the milk and slowly add it to the roux, whisking continuously. The mixture will start to thicken and resemble a white sauce. Once all the milk has been added, continue to stir for about 5 minutes, over a low heat, until the sauce thickens.

Add the mint, basil, salt, pepper, lemon zest and juice, grate in the hard cheese, and cook until the cheese has been incorporated into the sauce (about 3 minutes),

stirring continuously. Taste and season with salt and pepper, then take out 2 ladlefuls of the béchamel and put aside for the top of the lasagne.

Put the cooked broccoli, courgette and squash into a large bowl and add the spinach and crumbled feta. Add the rest of the béchamel and mix together.

Half fill a family-size baking dish with the veg and béchamel mix, smooth it level, and cover with a layer of lasagne sheets. Add the remaining half of the veg and béchamel mix and cover with a second layer of lasagne. Add a final layer of béchamel (the ladlefuls that you put aside earlier), then grate the Cheddar and spread on top.

Bake in the oven for about 30 minutes, until golden.

# HAPPY PEAR MOUSSAKA  SERVES 8

A really hearty, substantial dish to make an occasion for! It takes a while to prepare and cook, but it's worth the effort. Fantastic on a cold winter's night with a simple green salad and a glass of red wine. This recipe makes eight hearty portions, so if you're not eating it all at once, you get the pleasure of eating it for a couple of days and the flavours only improve. It freezes well too.

- 1 clove of garlic
- 1 medium red pepper
- 2 medium onions
- 1 carrot
- 400g Puy lentils, or other brown or green lentils
- a bunch of fresh thyme (or 1 tablespoon dried thyme if you don't have fresh)
- a bunch of fresh parsley
- 4 sprigs of rosemary
- 1 bay leaf
- 2 tablespoons paprika
- 1 x 400g tin of chopped tomatoes
- 10 tablespoons tamari
- salt and freshly ground black pepper
- 3 medium aubergines
- a pinch of cayenne pepper
- 500g potatoes
- 1 tablespoon oil
- 150g Cheddar cheese

Preheat the oven to 200°C/400°F/gas mark 6.

Peel and crush or finely slice the garlic. Deseed and finely chop the red pepper. Peel and finely chop the onions. Cut the carrot into small rounds.

Put the lentils into a large pan with the garlic, red pepper, onion, carrot and 1 litre of water and place, uncovered, on a high heat. Add a bouquet garni (see page 220) of the thyme, parsley, rosemary and bay leaf (or if you prefer you can add the herbs direct to the pan, taking the leaves off the stalks). Bring to the boil, then turn the heat down, add the paprika, tinned tomatoes, 5 tablespoons of the tamari, 1 teaspoon of salt and ½ teaspoon of black pepper, and simmer for about 30 minutes, until the lentils are cooked and nearly all the water has evaporated. Taste and add more salt and pepper if necessary.

Meanwhile, cut the aubergines into 1cm thick rounds and put them into a bowl. Add the remaining 5 tablespoons of tamari, 3 tablespoons of water and a pinch of cayenne, and mix together. Once the aubergines are coated, spread them out on a baking tray.

Slice the unpeeled potatoes into 1cm thick rounds, put them on another baking tray, and toss with 1 tablespoon of oil and 1 teaspoon of salt. Bake the aubergines and potatoes in the oven for 25 minutes, or until tender (if you prefer, the sliced potatoes can also be boiled). Remove from the oven but don't turn it off.

## For the béchamel sauce

- 750ml dairy or non-dairy milk
- 1 bay leaf
- 1 teaspoon grated or ground nutmeg
- 1½ teaspoons salt
- ½ teaspoon freshly ground black pepper
- 115g butter or 115ml oil
- 115g white spelt or wheat flour
- 2 eggs (optional)
- 350g yoghurt
- 100g grated Cheddar cheese

Now make the sauce. Put the milk, bay leaf, nutmeg, salt and pepper into a medium pan on a medium heat, stirring occasionally. In another pan, melt the butter or heat the oil gently over a low heat. Whisk the flour into the fat for about 5 minutes, until it is absorbed. You will have a thick paste (a roux).

Once the milk begins to bubble, take it off the heat. Remove the bay leaf. Slowly add the milk to the roux, whisking continuously. The mixture will start to thicken and resemble a white sauce. Once all the milk has been added, continue to stir for about 5 minutes, over a low heat, until the sauce thickens.

If using the eggs, add them one at a time, whisking continuously, and beat them into the sauce. Stir in the yoghurt. Remove from the heat, season to taste, and finally add the 100g of grated cheese.

To assemble the moussaka, start by putting the potatoes in the base of a large family-size ovenproof dish. Spread one-third of the white sauce on top. Remove the bouquet garni from the lentil mix, then, using a slotted spoon (to avoid excess liquid), add half to the dish. Now lay on half the aubergines, followed by another layer of white sauce. You should be about halfway up the dish by now.

Sprinkle slightly less than half the remaining grated cheese over the white sauce, then spoon the remaining lentil mixture on top. Follow with the rest of the aubergines and another layer of white sauce.

Finally, grate the 150g of Cheddar cheese and sprinkle it on top and bake in the oven for 30–40 minutes. We usually leave it to stand for 5–10 minutes out of the oven before serving, so that it 'sets'.

Great with a simple green salad of rocket, tossed leaves, sliced cucumber and sliced tomato, with a light lemon and olive oil dressing.

# ROASTED MEDITERRANEAN VEG AND LOCAL CHEDDAR LASAGNE SERVES 8

A staple dish that ten years after we opened is still one of the favourites! The veg used are totally interchangeable with whatever your preferences. It's the roasted garlic and sun-dried tomatoes that make the tomato sauce stand out from the crowd.

- 1 red pepper
- 1 yellow pepper
- 2 red onions
- 1 courgette
- 2 aubergines
- 1 bulb of fennel
- 4 tablespoons olive oil
- 2 tablespoons balsamic vinegar
- 2 teaspoons salt

**For the tomato sauce**
- 1 onion
- 1 bulb of garlic
- 2 tablespoons oil
- 3 x 400g tins of chopped tomatoes
- 2 bay leaves
- leaves from a few sprigs of fresh thyme or 2 teaspoons dried thyme (optional)
- 1 teaspoon salt
- ½ teaspoon freshly ground black pepper
- 8 sun-dried tomatoes

Preheat the oven to 200°C/400°F/gas mark 6.

Deseed the peppers, peel the red onions, and cut both into bite-size pieces, along with the courgette, aubergines and fennel. Put all the prepared veg into a large mixing bowl and add the olive oil, balsamic vinegar and salt. Mix thoroughly, then spread the veg out on a baking tray (you may need two trays) and roast in the oven for 25–30 minutes.

Meanwhile make the tomato sauce. Peel and finely chop the onion. Cut the top off the garlic bulb and remove some of the white outer skin to show the tips of the cloves. Cover it with tin foil and roast it with the veg for about 30 minutes.

Put 2 tablespoons of oil into a large family-size pan over a medium heat. Add the chopped onion, then reduce the heat and leave to cook gently for 10 minutes with the lid on, stirring occasionally. Add the tinned tomatoes, bay leaves, thyme (if you have some), salt, pepper and sun-dried tomatoes and stir them in. Bring to the boil, then reduce to a simmer.

Once the garlic is ready, squeeze the insides of the cloves into the tomato sauce. Remove the bay leaves and blend the sauce. Leave to simmer, and once the vegetables in the oven are done, stir them into the blended tomato sauce. Leave the oven turned on.

CD CG NV

### For the béchamel sauce

- 800ml milk
- 100g butter or 80ml sunflower or other neutral-tasting oil
- 80g plain white or spelt flour
- 50g Cheddar cheese
- 1 teaspoon salt
- ½ teaspoon freshly ground black pepper
- 1 teaspoon grated nutmeg

### To assemble

- 200g lasagne sheets
- 150g Cheddar cheese

To make the béchamel, put the milk into a medium pan on a medium heat, stirring occasionally. In another pan, melt the butter or heat the oil gently over a low heat. Whisk the flour into the fat for about 5 minutes, until the flour is absorbed. You will be left with a thick paste (a roux).

As the milk comes to the boil (it should be ready at about the same time as the roux), take it off the heat and add it to the roux a little at a time, whisking continuously. Once all the milk has been added, continue to stir for 5–10 minutes, over a low heat, until the sauce thickens. Remove from the heat, grate in the cheese and season with the salt, black pepper and nutmeg.

Make a layer of béchamel (about one-fifth of the sauce) in the bottom of a large family-size baking dish and cover with a layer of lasagne sheets. Add half the tomato and veg sauce and spread out evenly. Cover with another layer of lasagne sheets, then spread over half the remaining béchamel. Grate 50g of the Cheddar over the béchamel, then spread over the remaining tomato and veg sauce.

Add a final layer of lasagne, followed by the remaining béchamel. Scatter the rest of the grated Cheddar on top and bake in the oven for about 30 minutes, until golden.

# AUBERGINE PARMIGIANA SERVES 6

Our dear friend Luca D'Alfonso introduced us to this dish at his place one day and since then it has been a regular on our menu. This is our take on this super-tasty dish. It's a good one.

5 large aubergines • 1 onion • 6 sun-dried tomatoes • 2 x 400g tins of chopped tomatoes, or 1kg fresh ripe tomatoes • 6 tablespoons olive oil • 3 teaspoons salt • 1 bulb of garlic • 2 bay leaves • 5 sprigs of fresh thyme (optional) • 1 heaped teaspoon dried oregano • leaves from 1 small sprig of fresh oregano (optional) • freshly ground black pepper, to taste • 1 teaspoon white wine vinegar • 150g full-flavoured hard cheese, e.g. vegetarian style Parmesan or mature Cheddar • 25g fresh basil

Cut the aubergines lengthwise into long, thin strips. Peel and roughly chop the onion. Cut the sun-dried tomatoes into small pieces and finely chop the fresh tomatoes (if using).

Preheat the oven to 200°C/400°F/gas mark 6.

Put the aubergine strips into a bowl with 4 tablespoons of olive oil and 2 good pinches of salt and mix to coat. Put on a baking tray and roast in the oven for 25 minutes, then put aside, leaving the oven turned on. While the aubergines are roasting, cut the top off the garlic bulb and remove some of the white outer skin to show the tips of the cloves. Cover it with tin foil and roast it with the aubergines in the oven for 25–30 minutes.

Put 2 tablespoons of oil into a large family-size pan over a medium heat. Add the chopped onions and stir for 1 minute. Then reduce the heat and cook gently for 10 minutes with the lid on. Add the tinned or fresh tomatoes, bay leaves, thyme leaves (if you have some), dried oregano, fresh oregano (if using) and sun-dried tomatoes and stir them in. Bring to the boil, then reduce the heat to a simmer.

When the garlic is done, take it out of the oven and squeeze the insides of the cloves into the tomato sauce. Remove the bay leaves and blend the sauce until it is reasonably smooth. Season with salt, black pepper and white wine vinegar and leave to simmer away gently.

Grate the cheese. Put a thin layer of the tomato sauce in the bottom of a family-size oven dish, followed by a single layer of aubergines, a layer of basil leaves and a layer of grated cheese. Repeat the layers (leaving enough cheese to sprinkle on top) until the dish is full, then bake in the oven for 25 minutes.

# SPANISH CHICKPEA AND POTATO BAKE SERVES 6

A favourite on the menu. What really makes it stand out is if you stir some sun-dried tomato pesto into the stew as well as putting it on top after you bake it – we highly recommend this! A topping of grated Cheddar is lovely too.

- 1 onion
- 2 cloves of garlic
- 1 fresh chilli or ½ teaspoon chilli powder
- 1 stick of celery
- 2 carrots
- 1 green pepper, deseeded
- 2 leeks
- 700g potatoes
- 2 tablespoons olive oil
- 1 bay leaf
- 2 teaspoons mixed herbs
- 1 teaspoon paprika
- ½ teaspoon smoked paprika (optional)
- 1 tablespoon tomato purée
- 1 x 400g tin of chopped tomatoes
- 1 x 400g tin of chickpeas
- 50g parsley
- 1 tablespoon honey or other natural sweetener
- 1 tub of sun-dried tomato pesto

Peel and chop the onion and garlic. Deseed and chop the fresh chilli (if using). Cut the celery, carrots, pepper and leeks (green parts too) into bite-size pieces. Cut the potatoes into thin slices.

Put the oil into a large pan on a low to medium heat and add the onions and bay leaf. Cook the onions gently for about 10 minutes, stirring regularly, until they are soft and translucent. Add the garlic, celery, carrots and the fresh chilli (if using) and continue to cook for 6–8 minutes, stirring regularly, and adding a small amount of water if the vegetables begin to dry out.

Add the dried herbs, spices, pepper and leeks and cook for a further 5 minutes on a medium heat, stirring regularly. Now stir in the tomato purée, followed by the tinned tomatoes. Turn up the heat and bring to boiling point, then reduce the heat to a gentle simmer. Drain and rinse the chickpeas and add to the pan, then leave to simmer for 10–15 minutes. Meanwhile, steam or boil the potatoes.

Preheat the oven to 200°C/400°F/gas mark 6.

Chop the parsley and add most of it to the chickpea stew along with the honey. Season to taste with salt and freshly ground black pepper.

Pour the stew into a casserole dish and top with the sliced potatoes, overlapping them slightly. Sprinkle with salt and drizzle with olive oil, then bake in the oven for about 20–25 minutes, until the stew is bubbling and the potatoes are crispy.

To serve, lightly spread sun-dried tomato pesto over the potatoes and garnish with the rest of the parsley.

# THE HAPPY PEAR
# COMMUNITY

A few years ago we decided to sell porridge every morning. We were making it for ourselves and staff most mornings anyhow, so why not sell it too? We didn't know what to charge, and we weren't really sure if people would still want to eat porridge after 9 a.m., so we decided a good way to see if people were into porridge was to give it away for free for two weeks. If people wouldn't eat it for free, then they sure as heck weren't going to pay for it! We made up a fruit compote and granola to go with it and decided to charge a euro for the toppings.

At the end of the week, Steve said, 'I enjoyed giving that away for free so much, let's keep doing it!' Dave agreed and that was it! Every morning (Mon-to-Fri) for the last three years we have made organic porridge and given it away for free. Most customers get compote and granola on it and pay the massive sum of €1 for their brekkie!

Often fifteen minutes after opening, upstairs is brimming with people chatting over their hot porridge. It has been a lovely thing to do. People are delighted to get a healthy, tasty brekkie for free or for a euro and it puts them in good humour. It doesn't cost us a lot to do and the benefits and rise in all-round friendliness and niceness far outweigh the cost! We are also part of the suspended coffee movement, where someone prepays for a coffee for someone who may need one. If someone was out without any money they could pop in and order a 'suspended coffee'. We have a little blackboard showing the tally of prepaid coffees we have on offer. When they read our sign, customers love to support it and prepay for a coffee for someone they don't know!

Doing the morning porridge, or giving people the opportunity to buy a coffee for someone they don't know who may need it, is exactly what we mean when we talk about community. We grew up in Greystones, and when we started the Happy Pear it was so natural for us to embrace the local community and try to contribute to it in some way. From early on we really wanted this to be part of how we did business. It seemed to us that society has become so busy and disparate that people can feel very isolated. But when given the opportunity to connect with their neighbours, people are actually surprised at how much they enjoy themselves.

Sometimes we've had phone calls from strangers at 10 at night, people who have somehow managed to get one of our numbers and got in touch to say that the front door of the shop is wide open but it looks like the rest of the place is locked up for the night. We've obviously gone off without closing the door and a stranger knew how to find us to tell us. That sort of thing gives us a good feeling and really represents being part of the community, everyone helping each other!

We try to buy as much fruit and veg off as many local veg enthusiasts as we can, often trading them their home-grown stuff for some groceries. Keeping things local is where it's at as far as we are concerned. A friend came back from travelling flat broke in the middle of the recession and immediately lined himself up with a couple of weeks' painting work. He says the more friends you have the more recession-proof you are. His experience bears out exactly what we think. And we believe it's the same with a business: the more you involve yourself and give to the local community the more it insulates your business from recession.

About two years after we opened, there must have been a bumper harvest of apples because out of the blue lots of different people dropped in boxes of cooking apples: they had too many to use and said they knew we would make good use of them. Before long we were swimming in apples. We started giving them away and then a lovely lady said she would make us an apple pie to say thanks. Then another lady said the same thing and we bantered with her about whether her apple pie would be as good as the previous lady's! One of us then came up with the idea of having an apple-pie-baking competition to celebrate all the local apples. We set a date for a Sunday afternoon in early October, did up lots of posters, put it on the board out front and even put a notice in the local parish bulletins. With great originality, we called it our 'Local Apple Pie Baking Contest'! We gave all the apples away to promote it and to build a bit of hype. We also asked a mix of people to be judges – a couple of lovely older ladies (defo the apple pie experts!), a couple of teenagers and a few in-between – a real cross-section.

The day came and the sun shone and we had about thirty entries in all different shapes, styles and sizes. We had lots of kids entering, so we did a kids' section too. We asked local friends who were musicians to play some tunes in exchange for free coffee and food. The judges tasted all the pies, selected two winners, and we gave them a voucher for a prize and then everyone descended on all the entries in true celebration of apple pie. And we had such fun that first year that the pie-making contest has become an annual event!

After that we decided to have other baking competitions throughout the year, mainly in the milder months. Usually we have a 'Chocolate Love Fest' – a competition for all things chocolatey that is very keenly contested! We have also had brown bread, summer fruit cake, flapjack, banana bread and even pumpkin-carving competitions. There are usually as many kids' entries as adults. We have had some incredible entries over the years and it really creates a sense of fun. The point is just to have a bit of craic and a family day out at the front of the shop in celebration of good homemade seasonal food. There's live music and hordes of families and all sorts of folk soaking up the atmosphere. On one particularly memorable occasion, someone brought along a wood-burning hot-tub to set up out front of the shop. After the baking competition, some brave souls stripped off and hopped into a hot-tub in the heart of the main street of Greystones on a Sunday afternoon! What cheer!

## OUR BAKING COMPETITIONS REALLY CREATE A SENSE OF FUN.

Maybe a year into our adventure, a friend was selling an old hot-dog wagon and Dave thought it would be great fun to buy it, turn it into a smoothie wagon and bring the show on the road. It was pretty much a fancy old horsebox with two little skinny wheels that didn't really look like they would keep it up! We wanted to go to some music festivals and we loved work, so we thought why not marry the two together and see what happened! We spent the summer of 2006 getting it ready in the yard out back. First up was Electric Picnic – we signed up as traders and took our juice wagon off on its maiden voyage to Stradbally, Co. Laois, and made it the whole way there without any real drama.

On the first day, Steve and Kev (our childhood friend who was helping us) had the idea of selling smoothies with nothing on but aprons, so every time someone came to buy a smoothie from the front they saw two lads wearing aprons, but once they turned around to make the smoothie they were presented with two white arses! Possibly not the most hygienic of things to do, but it was a laugh. This little stunt got loads of attention and the queues grew longer and longer till a Garda came along and put the end to it! We had hordes of people around the next day looking to see the show too!

We did OK at that first Electric Picnic, and we had a ball, so we thought, 'Let's jump into this and give it a good go.' Kev said he would run it so we set up a company between the three of us and off we went.

The next summer we signed up to every music festival going. We had a laugh but lost lots of money. We learned we had to be a bit more selective with what festivals to do – and that Irish people don't buy smoothies in the rain! And as for fruit … At Oxegen one year we decided to take a second stall, in addition to our smoothie wagon. Since we were trying to make fruit and veg seem cool and attractive, and music festivals were always seen as cool and attractive, we thought it was a match made in heaven: we'd sell fruit at Oxegen and people would gobble it up! So we bought a load of stock and off we went.

We returned home with a van full of rotting strawberries and fermenting water-melons. Lesson learned: even at cool music festivals, drunk people prefer chips and pizza to strawberries!

Quite fittingly, at the end of our second season doing festivals, the wheels literally started to fall off the wagon! Steve remembers driving down to Stradbally and about two miles out he saw a wheel shoot past him into the bushes. He looked in the back mirror and saw sparks shooting up as the axle of our wagon dragged on the ground. Steve burst out laughing – it was that or burst into tears! To make a long story short, he eventually made it to the festival but after that we knew our festival days were numbered. A couple of years later, we had had enough of our mobile smoothie horsebox so we had a big bonfire and burned it down on a friend's farm!

For the last five years, the Zimmer Swimmers have been a part of the Happy Pear. They are a group of wonderful men and women, most over the age of 50, some in their 70s and even 80s, who swim in the sea every day, all year round, rain, sleet, sun and snow. They are hard-core! Watching them on the beach is a joy, as they know how to have fun and regularly play tricks on one another! The Happy Pear has become kind of like their clubhouse and they come up for hot soup and coffee after their dip. To us they represent 'the good life'; they not only swim in the sea daily – something dear to our hearts – but they take the time in the middle of the day to spend time together over lunch when everyone around them is busy as bees.

We have built a really decent online community on Facebook and Twitter (indeed, at the 2013 Restaurant Association of Ireland awards we won the award for best digital marketing). Back when Dave's first daughter, Elsie, was born he was out walking her back to sleep around by the sea at 5 a.m. There happened to be a really nice sunrise and he took a photograph of it and put it up on Facebook. People really liked the photo. Elsie is nearly four now, and ever since then we still take lots of photos of the sunrise and put them up. People really like them and we love to do it too!

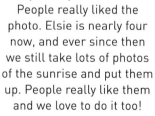

Karma means
you dont get away
with anything!

Veggie Stew

BEHIND THE SCEN
The HAPPY P
ORGANIC INGREDIENTS WE

On the other end of the age range, since we started we've been going to some of the local primary schools every year with our 'Smoothie Road Show'. It is usually during Healthy Eating Week and the idea is to inspire the kids to eat more fruit and veg.

We have a ball! Usually we set up in the big hall and we get to see all the kids from the whole school over the course of the day. It's exhilarating, exhausting and a hoot all at the same time! It's a bit like being a court jester in that you have to work hard to keep the kids' attention and to keep it fun. It's amazing how some kids can tell you what samphire is and what a fig looks like and they really know their produce, and then there are other kids that think a leek is a sword and anything outside of apples, carrots, bananas and potatoes is unknown!

In one of the games we divide the kids into two groups and put them head-to-head. We then get both groups to pick from loads of different fruits and veg and make a smoothie and come up with a name. Some groups make nice sweet fruity ones, and then other groups (usually the boys) put in chillies, onions and even cabbage and can get very 'creative' about it! We get the teachers to judge in front of all the kids. We really milk it and the kids go wild!

Other fun stuff we do? Well, there is a film club that a movie guru friend, Paul Byrne, runs in our café a few times a month. And of course the Happy Heart courses, which are lots of fun as well as having a serious purpose.

As part of our responsibility to be an example in our community of what a business can be and do, we also want to show the next generation how life can be fun and enjoyable. We want them to see that work can be an adventure and doesn't have to be all toil. Each year we take on more and more kids for work experience from transition year in school. We regularly have people volunteering in our kitchens to learn more about how to cook more healthily.

Over the last ten years we have had a fantastic community of people work with us, all coming for different reasons and for different lengths of time, from all parts of the world and also from just up the road. We have always done our best to create an atmosphere where staff enjoy coming to work, where there is fun, and – not to sound soppy – where there's a family-type feel, a work family. We feel this is super-important. We all spend lots of time at work so it is fundamental that staff enjoy being here, that though they may not enjoy every aspect of their job they enjoy being a part of the journey.

In the early years, we only employed friends or people that we wanted as friends! For a while it was the 'Spanish Inquisition', where we had Carmen, Jose and Borja and other wonderful Spaniards playing shop with us. We all learned to speak pretty good Spanish and I think we had as many people able to speak Spanish as not by the end of our Spanish chapter.

We have been very fortunate to have brilliant chefs with us right since we started who share our love of the veg! Let us introduce you to some of our fantastic team – you'll see their names on many of the recipes – recipes they have either devised, trialled or perfected.

**Dorene a.k.a. Lady Palmer:** Dorene has been cooking with us from Day One. She has 30 years' experience cooking this way and is very fluid and instinctive in the kitchen. As well as that, she is a beautiful shiny lady who is a joy to work with. Dorene's last meal would be Dahl with ripe avocado and toasted pitta bread soldiers (page 104)!

**Claire McCormick:** Since Claire can conjure up food that a mere mortal just can't, Dorene has called her a 'culinary witch'! She has an incredible palate and she is perhaps the most creative chef we have met. Anywhere there is smoked paprika in the recipes, that's probably Claire's work! Claire has cooked and taught veggie cookery for over 20 years. Her last meal would be Samphire, Cider and Veg Chowder (page129).

**Phil Smith a.k.a. The Ninja:** Phil works like a ninja, with precision, grace and ease. He is so wonderfully professional and manages all the nuts and bolts of our kitchens. Most of the 'burger' type mains are his and he is also a great man for the curries. Phil's last meal would be Beetroot, Walnut and Feta Burgers with Roasted Carrot Hummus (page 130).

**Michelle Hunt:** Michelle is queen of healthy sweet stuff. A good few of the desserts are Shel's creations. One of the loveliest things about when Shel works is that she usually brings in a plate full of her latest creations for whoever is working to taste and share. Thank you, Shel! Her last meal would be a frittata followed by a Healthy Chocolate-coated 'Caramel' Bar (page 180).

**Sally Marshall:** The wonderful Sally Marshall was our first head baker and she set the tone for all our baking. Lots of the recipes we still use today she came up with. She was also our first manager and did an awesome job. She now lives in Oz – we miss you, Sally! Sally's last meal would be Happy Pear White Lasagne (page 142).

**He Qiang a.k.a. Master of the Salads:** He Qiang is a salad chef with a great eye for colour and detail. You always know when He Qiang is working, as the salad bar is bursting with more contrasting colours than usual. His last meal would be Roasted Mediterranean Veg and Local Cheddar Lasagne (page 148).

**Jennifer Rooney and Ola Radyno:** Our baking supremos! Both wonderful women who do a fantastic job. We are lucky to have such bakers. They are always up for trying something new and are great fun to work with. Jen's last meal would be Tasty Veg Bake in a Roasted Red Pepper Cream Sauce (page 139) and Ola's would be Happy Pear Moussaka (page 144).

deliciously indulgent

# DESSERTS, CAKES AND SWEET TREATS

be good to yourself

go on... treat yourself

sweet tooth?

# CHOCOLATE MOUSSE CAKE MAKES 10 SLICES

Our most popular cake by far. This is a great recipe, really gooey, intensely chocolatey, with a crunchy exterior. It really is hard to beat – a very satisfying cake!

- 165g sunflower margarine
- 265g organic caster sugar
- a small pinch of salt
- 300g dark chocolate (53% Belgian drops are perfect)
- 5 eggs
- 70g ground almonds
- a small handful of roughly chopped or flaked almonds

Preheat your oven to 170°C/325°F/gas mark 3.

Prepare a 23cm round non-stick springform cake tin by putting a layer of baking parchment on the bottom and then putting the bottom and sides together, cutting away excess parchment sticking out to about 1cm around the edge. The other option with these is to use a muffin tray and cases to make little mousse muffins, which are really quite lovely.

Put the margarine into a heatproof bowl set over a pan of simmering water and add the sugar and salt. Stir until the margarine has melted, then turn off the heat and add the chocolate, stirring until it too has melted. Take the bowl off the heat and leave to cool.

Beat the eggs and ground almonds for about 4 minutes, until light, fluffy and creamy. Add to the cooled chocolate mixture and stir until combined.

Pour into your prepared tin and sprinkle the almonds on top. Bake for 35–40 minutes – like brownies, you want the top crunchy but the centre dense and gooey.

Leave the cake in the tin for about 30 minutes before attempting to take it out, as it will be soft and inclined to crack otherwise.

If you are making mousse muffins, the baking time will drop to about 25–30 minutes.

# CHOCOLATE, ORANGE AND GINGER CAKE
## MAKES 10–12 SLICES

A soft, rich, chocolatey, gluten-free cake. This has been on our menu for more than five years and has a very loyal following.

- 3 small oranges (ideally organic)
- 6 eggs
- 200g ground almonds
- 250ml agave syrup or 250g sugar
- 100g cocoa powder (depending on how rich you want it)
- 1 teaspoon baking powder
- ½ teaspoon bread soda/ bicarbonate of soda
- zest of 2 oranges
- 2 teaspoons ground ginger
- 3 heaped teaspoons grated fresh ginger (add more or less to personal taste)

Put the whole oranges into a pan, cover them with water, and boil for 2 hours, making sure they are always fully submerged in the water. Remove from the water and leave to cool (we find if we cut them in half they cool a lot quicker).

Preheat your oven to 170°C/325°F/gas mark 3. Prepare a 20cm round non-stick springform cake tin by putting a layer of baking parchment on the bottom and then putting the bottom and sides together, cutting away excess parchment sticking out to about 1cm around the edge.

Blend the cooled boiled oranges into a smooth pulp in a food processor, making sure to remove any pips first. Add the agave syrup (save a little to spread on top of the cake once cooked). In a separate bowl whisk the eggs and ground almonds. Combine the orange and egg mixes together.

Sift the cocoa, baking powder and bread soda/ bicarbonate of soda into a bowl and mix together lightly. Pour in the orange and egg mixture, add the orange zest, ground ginger and grated fresh ginger, and stir to combine. Pour the cake mix into the prepared cake tin and bake for about 50 minutes, or until a skewer inserted into the middle comes out clean.

Pour the reserved agave syrup over the cake and leave in the tin for 10–15 minutes before removing. Decorate with orange zest.

# COURGETTE AND LEMON CURD CAKE 10–12 SLICES

This is one of our most popular cakes – a favourite recipe from our first manager, the great Sally Marshall. It's a lovely fresh-tasting cake with a curd filling that brightens up even the dullest day. If possible put the cake into the fridge for a little while before cutting. Otherwise you may find the curd squidges out the sides a bit!

500g organic courgettes • 450g white spelt flour or regular plain flour, plus extra for dusting • 2 teaspoons baking powder • 1 teaspoon bread soda/bicarbonate of soda • 250g organic caster sugar • 250ml sunflower oil • 3 eggs
**For the curd** • 50g sunflower margarine • 2 eggs • 50g organic caster sugar • 80ml lemon or lime juice
**For the icing and decoration** • 50g unsalted butter • 1 tablespoon honey or agave syrup, to taste • 100g Philadelphia cheese • zest of 1 lemon and 1 lime

Preheat the oven to 170°C/325°F/gas mark 3. Lightly grease two sandwich cake tins and dust them with flour.

Coarsely grate the courgettes without peeling them – if there is a lot of liquid coming off them, drain them in a colander or sieve.

Sift the flour, baking powder and bread soda/bicarbonate of soda into a bowl. Beat the sugar, oil and eggs in another bowl until smooth and creamy. Add to the flour, beat gently, then add the courgettes and mix carefully.

Pour into the cake tins. Bake for 50 minutes, or until a skewer inserted into the middle comes out clean. Leave for 10–15 minutes, then turn out on to a rack to cool.

To make the curd, melt the margarine over a very low heat. Add the rest of the ingredients and whisk constantly until it starts to thicken to a custard-type consistency. It is very important to keep the heat low, to avoid scrambled eggs! Leave to cool.

To make the icing, cut the butter into cubes, put it into a blender with the honey and blend until smooth and creamy – you may need to stop the machine and scrape down the ingredients a few times before it is all mixed. Add the Philadelphia gradually until it's all in. Check the level of sweetness in the icing and add more honey if you want it sweeter. Don't over-mix the icing or it will end up going runny.

Allow the cakes to cool, then cut the top off one of them to flatten it and generously spread the cut surface with the curd. (Any leftover curd can be kept in a jar in the fridge.) Spread the icing over the rounded top of the other cake. Carefully position the second cake on top of the curd and sprinkle with lemon and lime zest.

# BANANA AND WALNUT CAKE MAKES 7 SLICES

We have been making this for years. It's another super recipe by Sally Marshall that is very straightforward to make. It's a real popular seller in the café and goes great in the afternoon with a nice cup of tea!

- 100g raisins
- 200g white spelt flour, plus extra for dusting
- 1½ teaspoons ground cinnamon
- 2 teaspoons baking powder
- ½ teaspoon bread soda/ bicarbonate of soda
- 120ml sunflower oil
- 150g honey
- 2 large eggs
- 2 medium bananas
- 50g walnuts

Preheat your oven to 150°C/300°F/gas mark 2. Lightly grease a 900g loaf tin with margarine and dust it with spelt flour.

Put the raisins into a small pan, cover with water and bring to the boil. Turn off the heat and set aside until you need them.

Sift the flour, cinnamon, baking powder and bread soda/bicarbonate of soda into a large bowl and mix together. In a jug mix the sunflower oil, honey and eggs until combined. Whiz the bananas in a blender or food processor and add them to the jug.

Now pour the wet ingredients from the jug into the bowl of dry ingredients and mix until smooth. Drain the raisins and stir in along with the walnuts. (Generally we would crush the walnuts a little in our hands first; it's also nice to save a few for the top, to go crunchy.)

Pour the mixture into your prepared loaf tin, throw the reserved walnuts on top and bake for about 1 hour and 15 minutes, or until a skewer comes out nearly clean.

Leave to cool for 10–15 minutes, then turn out into a wire rack to cool.

Banana cake is lovely by itself or, if you're feeling a bit more decadent, with some butter spread on it. If it gets a little stale you can toast it or put it into a warm oven for a little while and it will come out totally yummy again!

# AVOCADO CHOCOLATE MOUSSE CAKE
## MAKES 10–12 SLICES

A raw, sugar-free, dairy-free, egg-free and extremely tasty dessert. It keeps for five days in the fridge, and freezes very well. The ingredients are expensive, compared to typical cakes. However, it is rich, nourishing, satisfying and filling!

### For the base
- 300g almonds
- 300g cashew nuts
- 300g pitted dates (Medjool or regular)
- 2 tablespoons vanilla extract

### For the topping
- 4 ripe avocados
- ½ teaspoon sea salt
- 1 teaspoon cinnamon
- 4 tablespoons honey or agave syrup
- 90g cocoa powder
- ¾ teaspoon vanilla extract
- zest of 2 oranges

To make the base, blend the nuts, dates and vanilla extract together in a food processor until smooth and spread over the base of a 30cm baking tin, compacting it as you go.

To make the topping, put all the ingredients into a food processor or blender and press go until very smooth!

Spoon the chocolate mousse over the base, smoothing it out evenly, and leave to set in the fridge or freezer for 2 hours. (If you put it in the freezer allow it to thaw for a few minutes before serving.)

If you fancy it, you can decorate with berries before serving as we have here. We used fig as well. But the cake will be perfect without any pimping!

Now enjoy your healthy, sugar-free, delicious, wonderful, magnificent, delightful dessert!

# WHITE CHOCOLATE RASPBERRY CHEESECAKE SERVES 8

One of Shel's fantastic no-bake tarts – sweet, light, creamy, with a super-vibrant raspberry topping. The date and walnut base is really good too.

## For the base
- 180g pitted dates (Medjool or regular)
- 120g walnuts
- 100g regular or gluten-free oats, or almonds
- ½ teaspoon ground cinnamon
- 1–2 tablespoons orange juice
- 1 teaspoon vanilla extract

## For the filling
- 180g cashew nuts (soaked – see method opposite)
- 240ml unsweetened almond milk
- 1 tablespoon vanilla extract
- 100g xylitol or coconut sugar
- 1 tablespoon agar flakes (a healthy dairy-free setting agent; use the flakes, not the powder)
- 120g cacao butter

Cover the cashews in water and soak for a minimum of 4 hours. Ideally you would soak for up to 12 hours.

To make the base, put the dates into a food processor and blend to a smooth paste. Remove, then put the walnuts and oats or almonds into the processor and whiz to fine crumbs. Put the date paste back into the processor along with the cinnamon, orange juice and vanilla extract and process to combine. If necessary, add a little water so that the mixture forms a soft dough (but it shouldn't be sticky).

Press the dough into a 20cm round tin, preferably loose-bottomed. Using your hands, spread it evenly across the base and slightly up the sides. Refrigerate.

To make the filling, blend the soaked and drained cashews with 60ml of the almond milk and the vanilla extract in a blender or food processor to make a smooth cream. Blend in the xylitol or coconut sugar. Put the remaining almond milk into a pan over a medium heat. Bring to the boil, then sprinkle in the agar flakes, gently stir and leave to simmer for 3 minutes.

Meanwhile, put the cacao butter into a jug or jar and submerge it in a deep jug or bowl of boiling water to gently melt. Add the melted cacao butter to the milk and agar before pouring into the food processor and blending with the cashew cream. Pour into the tart base and return to the fridge for a minimum of 1 hour.

### For the topping

- 120g fresh raspberries
- 60ml fresh orange juice
- 50g xylitol, honey or maple syrup
- 2 tablespoons chia seeds
- 60g roughly chopped walnuts, for sprinkling over the top

To make the topping, place the raspberries, orange juice and xylitol, honey or maple syrup in a pan over a medium heat. Bring to the boil, then reduce to a simmer for 10–15 minutes. Mash to a chunky purée, place in a bowl, whisk in the chia seeds and put into the fridge alongside the tart.

Once the filling has set you can spread over the raspberry topping. Sprinkle the chopped walnuts on top. Put the cheesecake back into the fridge for at least 2 hours or overnight before gently removing from the tin and slicing.

Store in an airtight container in the fridge for 2–3 days, or freeze for up to 1 month.

# HEALTHY CHOCOLATE-COATED 'CARAMEL' BARS
## MAKES 10

The perfect homemade luxurious treat – a soft chewy almond base, a rich caramel filling and a dark chocolate coating (inspired by the iconic Twix™ bar). . . many people say these are better than the real thing!

### For the base
- 90g pitted dates (Medjool or regular)
- 240g ground almonds
- a pinch of salt
- 1 teaspoon vanilla extract

### For the filling
- 180g pitted dates (Medjool or regular)
- 90g cashew butter (or almond butter)
- 1 tablespoon water
- 1 tablespoon coconut oil

### For the chocolate coating
- 300g dark chocolate (70–85%)

To make the base of the bars, put the dates into a food processor and blend until smooth. If using regular dates, add a little water if needed to reach a nice thick paste. Add the ground almonds, salt and vanilla to the date paste.

When the base ingredients are fully mixed, shape into 20 bars about 7cm long and 0.5cm high and put them on a baking tray (one that will fit in your freezer!) lined with greaseproof or silicone paper. Place in the freezer. Leave them in for 15 minutes, as if the 'biscuit' layer isn't set it makes it harder to shape the rest.

In your processor, blend together the filling ingredients. While cashew butter is better, almond butter also works here. Again, if using regular dates, add a little water if needed to reach a nice thick paste. Remove the biscuit bases from the freezer and spread a thick layer of the date filling (the 'caramel' layer) over each one, smoothing the sides with a knife. Return to the freezer for at least 30 minutes.

Melt the chocolate in a bowl over a pan of simmering water, making sure the base of the bowl doesn't touch the water.

Remove the bars from the freezer. One at a time, roll them in the chocolate and put them back on the cold tray. The chocolate will harden almost instantly! Place in the fridge for an hour to firm up fully.

Store in the fridge.

# TIRAMISÙ SQUARES   MAKES 9 LARGE SQUARES

Almond milk, cashew cream, Baileys . . . creamy, slightly boozy deliciousness with a chewy chocolate and coffee-infused base – tiramisù never tasted so good.

### For the base
- 180g pitted dates (Medjool or regular)
- 100g gluten-free oats or almonds
- 60g hazelnuts
- 40g cocoa powder
- 1 tablespoon espresso powder or freshly ground coffee
- 1 teaspoon vanilla extract
- 1–2 tablespoons water

### For the vanilla layer
- 180g white cashew butter
- 90g pitted dates (Medjool or regular)
- 2 teaspoons vanilla extract
- 180ml unsweetened almond milk or any other non-dairy milk
- 1 tablespoon agar flakes (a healthy dairy-free setting agent; use the flakes, not the powder)

First make the base. Put the dates into a food processor and blend until smooth. If using regular dates, add a little water if needed to reach a nice thick paste. Remove, then put all the other base ingredients apart from the water into the processor and process to fine crumbs. Put the date paste back in and process to combine, adding 1–2 tablespoons of water – the dough should be firm and should come together in a ball in the processor.

Press the dough into a non-stick, loose-bottomed or silicone 20cm square tray, lined with baking parchment. Smooth out the surface. If you have a pastry roller, or even a narrow glass jar, you can use either to help roll it out evenly. Place in the fridge.

Now make the vanilla layer. In the processor, blend together the cashew butter, dates, vanilla and 1–2 tablespoons of the milk until perfectly smooth. Put the rest of the milk into a pan and bring to the boil, then sprinkle in the agar flakes and leave to simmer for 3 minutes. Quickly pour into the processor and blend with the cashew mixture.

Take the base out of the fridge and pour the cashew/vanilla mixture over, then smooth the surface and return it to the fridge. Leave to set for 30 minutes.

To make the cocoa/coffee layer, blend together the dates, cashew butter and 1–2 tablespoons of the freshly brewed coffee. Sift in the cocoa powder and process to combine, along with the vanilla extract and Baileys.

### For the cocoa/coffee layer

- 90g pitted Medjool dates
- 140g cashew butter
- 180ml freshly brewed strong coffee
- 1½ tablespoons cocoa powder
- 1 teaspoon vanilla extract
- 3 tablespoons Baileys, or other creamy liqueur of choice (if you need these to be 100% vegan, omit the Baileys or use a non-dairy liqueur!)
- 1 tablespoon agar flakes (a healthy dairy-free setting agent; use the flakes, not the powder)

### For the topping

- 20g dark chocolate (70–85%)

Place the rest of the coffee in a pan, bring to the boil, sprinkle in the agar flakes and leave to simmer for 3 minutes. Pour into the cocoa mixture and process to combine until smooth (just a minute or two).

Take the tray out of the fridge and pour the cocoa mixture over the set vanilla layer. Smooth out and return to the fridge for at least 4 hours, ideally overnight.

Grate the dark chocolate and sprinkle over, then gently remove from the tray. Slice up and serve. Store leftovers in the fridge for up to 3 days or freeze for up to 1 month.

# CASHEW BUTTER COOKIES MAKES 16

One of Shel's fantastic healthier desserts. These leave you wanting more! A simple recipe that Steve and his three-year-old daughter May often make.

- 240g 100% all-natural roasted cashew butter (almond or peanut butter will also work)
- 5 tablespoons coconut sugar
- 3 tablespoons maple syrup
- 1 teaspoon vanilla extract
- 2 tablespoons ground flaxseed/linseed
- ½ teaspoon bread soda/ bicarbonate of soda
- ½ teaspoon baking powder
- coarse sea salt (optional)

Put all the ingredients into a bowl and stir to combine. Place in the fridge for 30 minutes.

Preheat the oven to 200°C/400°F/gas mark 6.

Form the cookie dough into 16 balls, just smaller than golfball size. Press gently between the palms of your hands to slightly flatten (they will spread just a little while baking; the more you flatten them before baking, the thinner and flatter the cookies will be).

Place on a non-stick baking tray a few centimetres apart. Optional (but recommended!): sprinkle each with a pinch of coarse sea salt. Bake in the oven for 7–8 minutes for a soft, light, melt-in-the-mouth cookie – you can cook them for a couple of minutes longer for a crisper result.

Allow to cool for 5 minutes on the tray, then transfer to a wire rack to cool fully.

Store in an airtight container for up to 5 days.

# COCONUT MACAROONS MAKES 12–14

A lovely 'clean' treat that is simple to make, super-tasty and full of coconut. These store really well for a couple of weeks in a sealed container in the fridge – if you can resist that long!

- 120g unsweetened desiccated coconut
- 50g ground almonds
- 60ml maple syrup or honey
- 55g coconut oil, melted
- 1 teaspoon vanilla extract
- 60g dark chocolate (optional)

Preheat the oven to 140°C/275°F/gas mark 1 and line a baking tray with baking parchment.

Put the coconut and ground almonds into a bowl and mix together. In another bowl mix together the maple syrup or honey, melted coconut oil and vanilla extract.

Add the wet ingredients to the dry and stir well to combine. Using your hands or a melon ball scooper, create little tight, compact balls of the mixture and put them on the prepared baking tray.

Bake in the oven for 10 minutes, then remove and turn the tray around. Bake for a further 10 minutes, then turn the tray once more and bake for a further 5 minutes.

Allow to cool on the tray for 10 minutes before transferring to a wire rack to cool.

Meanwhile melt the chocolate (if using) in a heat-proof bowl set over a pan of boiling water, making sure the base of the bowl doesn't touch the water. Drizzle the macaroons with the chocolate.

# SHEL'S NO-BAKE CARAMEL SLICES MAKES 16

Shel's remake of one of our childhood classics – *thank you, Shel, for creating this!* This recipe is just as tasty as the condensed milk, sugar and shortbread classic that we devoured at kids' parties, but it's much healthier than our old favourite!

**For the base** • 360g pitted dates (Medjool or regular) • 220g regular or gluten-free oat flakes • 240g almonds • 2 teaspoons vanilla extract • 2 tablespoons coconut oil, melted
**For the filling** • 360g pitted dates (Medjool or regular) • 60g 100% all-natural smooth almond butter (or roasted cashew butter) • 110g coconut oil, melted • a pinch of sea or rock salt
**For the topping** • 200g dark dairy-free chocolate (preferably at least 70% cocoa solids) • 2 tablespoons coconut oil, melted

To make the base, put the dates into a food processor and blend until smooth. If using regular dates, add a little water if needed to reach a nice thick paste. Remove and set to one side. Put the oats and almonds into the processor and blend to fine crumbs. Break the date paste into chunks and add to the food processor, one chunk at a time. Add the vanilla and coconut oil and blend until you have crumbs that hold together when you press them between your fingers.

Place the mixture in a non-stick (ideally silicone) standard flapjack tray (30 x 20cm), lightly greased or lined with baking parchment. Spread evenly, pressing it down and compacting it with your hands or a pastry roller. Put into the fridge.

To make the caramel filling, put the dates into the food processor and blend until smooth. Again, if using regular dates add a little water if needed to reach a nice thick paste. Melt the almond or cashew butter with the coconut oil in a non-stick pan over a medium heat. Allow to cool for a couple of minutes, then add to the date paste in the food processor, along with the salt, and process to combine. Spread the filling over the base and return it to the fridge while you melt the chocolate for the topping.

Gently melt the chocolate in a heatproof bowl set over a pan of boiling water, making sure the base of the bowl doesn't touch the water. Remove from the heat, stir in the coconut oil, and pour over the caramel layer. Return to the fridge to set for at least 2 hours. Take your time to compact each layer before refrigerating, as this will ensure that it will not crumble and break when sliced later.

Remove from the fridge 30 minutes before slicing, to prevent the chocolate from cracking. Slice into 16 squares. Store any leftovers in an airtight container for up to 1 week, or freeze for up to 1 month.

# HAPPY PEAR FIG ROLLS MAKES 20

This is one of our wonderful cousin Naomi's recipes. It's a great take on the famous fig roll. These have a loyal following and you will see why when you taste the almond pastry. Now you know how to get the figs into the fig rolls!

### For the dough
- 380g ground almonds
- 40ml agave syrup
- 40ml sunflower oil
- 3 tablespoons vanilla extract

### For the filling
- 300g dried figs
- 75ml lemon juice
- 3 tablespoons vanilla extract

Put the figs into a food processor and blend until they are well chopped. Add the lemon juice and vanilla and process to a smooth paste. Put to one side.

Put the ground almonds into a bowl and add the rest of the dough ingredients. Mix well, then refrigerate the dough for 1 hour.

Preheat the oven to 150°C/300°F/gas mark 2.

Divide the chilled dough into four portions. Put one portion between two pieces of baking parchment and roll out into a 25cm x 10cm rectangle, 0.5cm thick. Spread a quarter of the filling evenly down the right-hand side (lengthwise) of the rectangle, then fold the other side of the dough over the filling – resulting in a 25cm x 5cm bar. Make the join where the dough meets tight and neat and as straight as possible.

Repeat with the three remaining portions of dough and the rest of the filling, transferring each bar to a baking sheet lined with baking parchment. Bake in the oven for 25–30 minutes, until golden brown, then remove and allow to cool for 10–15 minutes before cutting them into 5cm rolls – 20 fig rolls in total.

# GRAIN-FREE GRANOLA BARS MAKES 8 SMALL CHUNKY BARS

Lightly chewy, sweet, grain-free, nut-and-seed-loaded granola bars with a twist of fruit! A new weekly staple.

- 50g almonds
- 50g cashew nuts
- 30g sunflower seeds
- 100g dried fruit (we used figs and unsulphured apricots)
- 20g goji berries
- 30g desiccated coconut
- 40g pumpkin seeds
- ¼ teaspoon fine rock or sea salt
- 4 tablespoons coconut oil
- 60ml honey (or brown rice syrup if you want to make them vegan-friendly)
- 3 tablespoons 100% all-natural almond butter
- ½ teaspoon vanilla extract

Put the almonds, cashews and sunflower seeds into a food processor and blitz until finely chopped. Cut the dried fruit into small pieces. Put the nut/seed mix and dried fruit into a bowl. Add the goji berries, desiccated coconut and pumpkin seeds and mix well. Add the salt.

Melt the coconut oil in a bowl over a pan of simmering water over a medium heat. Once melted take it off the heat and add the honey, almond butter and vanilla extract. Combine well, using a fork or a small whisk.

Pour the wet ingredients on top of the dry ingredients and stir well to combine. Press the mixture into a 15–20cm square tray lined with baking parchment (choose your tin depending on the desired thickness of the bars – we use a 15cm square loose-bottomed tin).

Put into the fridge to set for 4 hours before slicing. Store in an airtight container in the fridge for up to 10 days, or freeze for up to 1 month.

192   desserts, cakes and sweet treats

# HONEY AND SEED FLAPJACKS MAKES 12

A lovely recipe from the wonderful Martha, who baked with us for a few years. This version will satisfy the most avid of flapjack lovers! A great addition to a lunchbox. If you want a gluten-free version of these flapjacks, use honey rather than barley malt.

- 150ml honey or barley malt
- 250g regular or gluten-free rolled oats
- 160ml sunflower oil
- 60g flax meal/ground flax seeds/linseed meal/ground linseeds (different names for the same thing!)
- 40g desiccated coconut
- 40g pumpkin seeds
- 40g sunflower seeds
- 40g sesame seeds
- 40g raisins
- 20g goji berries
- a pinch of salt

Preheat the oven to 180°C/350°F/gas mark 4.

Before you start, sit the jar of barley malt or honey in a bowl of hot water to heat it and make it more liquid.

Meanwhile, put the oats into a large bowl with the oil and stir to coat. Add all the remaining ingredients except the barley malt or honey and stir until everything is well mixed.

Add the barley malt or honey and mix thoroughly.

Roll the mixture out in a flapjack tin or on a flat baking tray to about 2.5cm thick. Bake for 25 minutes, then remove from the oven and leave to cool before cutting.

# SUPERFOOD TIFFINS  MAKES 16 MINI SQUARES

Another of Shel's delights! A great take on a tiffin, and the master version has all raw ingredients – though of course you can use whatever is accessible for you. Steve and his daughter May often make these. They look fantastic with the flecks of red goji berry and the white of the nuts.

- 140g cacao butter
- 6 tablespoons cacao powder
- 80g raw cashew butter/paste
- 6 tablespoons coconut sugar (or use granulated sugar if you're not concerned with keeping it raw)
- 6 tablespoons honey, maple syrup or agave syrup
- 2 teaspoons alcohol-free vanilla extract (or vanilla extract with alcohol, though this is not raw)
- 2 pinches of sea salt

### For the filling
- 60g walnut halves
- 60g raw cashew nuts
- 40g pitted figs
- 40g unsulphured dried apricots
- 60g dried mulberries or raisins
- 20g goji berries

Cut the cacao butter into small pieces and place in a bowl. Rest the bowl over a pan of simmering water (so it's not touching the water). Allow the cacao butter to melt slowly, stirring occasionally.

Meanwhile chop the walnuts, cashews, figs and apricots and mix in a bowl with the other filling ingredients. Spread the mixture evenly over the base of a non-stick silicone 20cm tray.

When the cacao butter is melted, mix in the cacao powder along with all the other chocolate ingredients and whisk until perfectly smooth. Cover the fruit and nut filling in the tray, pouring slowly and carefully to ensure it is evenly distributed. Give the tray a gentle shake, then transfer it to the fridge to firm up for at least 3 hours.

Allow to come to room temperature before slicing with a large sharp knife, using a see-saw motion to prevent cracking. Store the tiffins in an airtight container for up to 3 weeks.

# HAPPY PEAR NO-BAKE HEALTHY BROWNIES
## MAKES 9

Another of Shel's great recipes. These are super guilt-free snacks that come together with minimal effort and will satisfy nearly all chocolate cravings! They keep for at least 10 days in a sealed container in the fridge.

- 340g pitted dates (Medjool or regular)
- 110g regular or gluten-free oats, or extra nuts
- 60g almonds
- 60g walnuts
- 90g unsweetened cacao powder
- ¼ of a vanilla pod or 1 teaspoon vanilla extract

Put the dates into a food processor and blend until smooth. If using regular dates, add a little water if needed to reach a nice thick paste. Remove and set to one side. Put the oats, almonds and walnuts into the processor and blitz to form fine crumbs, then put the date paste back in, breaking it up into chunks.

Add the cacao powder, then either scrape the seeds from the vanilla pod into the bowl or add the vanilla extract and blend to combine. Add a little water if necessary, to create a dough that holds together when pressed between your fingertips.

Place the dough in a non-stick (ideally silicone) 20cm square baking tray, pressing it down with your hands to spread it evenly. If you have one, a pastry roller is handy to speed up the process. Or a small narrow jar. Place in the fridge for a couple of hours, then slice into 9 large brownies.

Store in an airtight container in the fridge for up to 10 days, or freeze for up to 1 month.

A high-energy wholefood snack that will satisfy your hunger and sweet tooth in one fell body-loving swoop!

- 200g almonds
- 45g pumpkin seeds
- 95g sunflower seeds
- 45g ground linseeds/flax seeds
- 40g sesame seeds
- 30g goji berries
- 60g dried apricots (preferably unsulphured)
- 50g desiccated coconut
- 35g cacao nibs
- 80g cacao butter
- 125ml raw honey (to make the bars vegan-friendly use brown rice syrup)
- 50g 100% all-natural almond butter
- ½ teaspoon salt
- ¼ of a vanilla pod (or if not concerned with keeping it raw, 1 teaspoon vanilla extract)

For the topping
- 50g cacao butter
- ½ a vanilla pod (or if not concerned with keeping it raw, 1 teaspoon vanilla extract)
- 55g cacao powder
- 70ml honey (maple, agave or brown rice syrup to make these vegan-friendly)
- desiccated coconut, to decorate

To make the base, place the nuts, seeds and dried fruit, plus the coconut and cacao nibs, in a food processor and blitz until everything is coarsely chopped.

Melt the cacao butter in a bowl set over a pan of simmering water. Put the honey, melted cacao butter, almond butter, salt and the seeds scraped from inside the vanilla pod into a bowl and whisk together, then add to the food processor and blitz for 2 minutes to combine. Using your hands, spread the mixture in a 23cm x 40cm tray, pressing it down firmly. Place in the fridge.

To make the topping, put the cacao butter into a heatproof bowl. Rest the bowl over a pan of boiling water and leave the butter to melt slowly, stirring frequently. You can set the bowl and pan on the stove top over a low heat, which will speed up the process slightly.

Once the cacao butter is melted, add the other topping ingredients and whisk to combine. Take the base out of the fridge and pour the topping over, spreading it evenly with a spatula or the back of a spoon. Place in the fridge to set for a minimum of 2 hours, but ideally overnight.

Slice into 16 even bars once set and decorate with desiccated coconut. Store in the fridge for up to 3 weeks in an airtight container or freeze for up to 3 months.

# OUR FIRST TEN YEARS

We have always loved games. When we were young we loved to play chasing and any kind of sport that was going. Business we have found to be the best game of the lot! We absolutely love it. We wake up excited, with a great sense of purpose to go forth and build our cathedral, one block at a time. At the core of what we do is that we want to enjoy ourselves and we want to have fun with those working with us and the customers that come in. We like to think that this atmosphere is part of what we have created, that it is a fun, open place. We don't tend to take things very seriously. We do our very best and usually things add up, and if they don't, well, hopefully they will tomorrow!

We started the Happy Pear on 26 November 2004. We both remember the day well. We were 24 and for a few months we had been getting ready for the off in the comfort of the family home, so we were raring to go. But nothing could have prepared us for what was ahead! We took over the shop on the Friday, closed for Saturday and Sunday and got to work on putting our stamp on the place. This was it! This was where we were going to make our mark in the universe, where our food revolution was going to start!

WE SAID THE BRIGHTEST COLOUR THEY HAD, OF COURSE, NEON PREFERABLY!
MUM WAS HORRIFIED — NONETHELESS, SHE CAME BACK WITH SOME PAINT
SAMPLES AND WE CHOSE THE BRIGHTEST ORANGE THEY HAD!

Not long into the demolition and makeover we needed to paint the front of the shop. Mum was in the thick of things, helping and supporting us as usual (thanks, Mum!). She said she would nip down to the Brady's Hardware and get the paint.

'What colour would we like? Cream? Or maybe white?'

We said the brightest colour they had, of course, neon preferably! Mum was horrified – what would her friends think? And what would the people in Greystones think? Nonetheless, she came back with some paint samples and we chose the brightest orange they had. It was either that or neon green. We wanted to make our dint in the world and we sure weren't going to be quiet about it!

We started with no business plan and no experience in retail. We didn't even know that much about fruit and veg, not to mind running a shop! We really weren't by the book at all. We knew we wanted to use business as a vehicle for social change but we didn't know how. All we had was this burning feeling inside us that we couldn't ignore, we had to follow it. We wanted to create a place that brought people together, that celebrated healthy food, that celebrated fresh fruits and veggies, and not to sound all cheesy, but a place that encouraged people to build a happier, healthier community. We were overflowing with enthusiasm and passion and we knew the first step was with our little shop.

When we first started we used to go into the fruit market at 4.30 a.m. wearing our shorts (all year round!) and bouncing around the market like a pair of young puppies, excited for another day playing shop. The lads who had been there for years used to laugh at us and say that the honeymoon would soon be over and we would be dragging ourselves around the market. Eventually they realized that we couldn't be suppressed! We weren't a flash in the pan and we were in it for the long haul.

In the early years of the shop we were both single and didn't have a lot of time to meet girls outside of work, so we nearly always met them through the shop. For dates, we would invite them to come along to the Dublin fruit and veg market at 4.30 a.m.! Over the years we brought lots of girls on a fruit and veg buying trip/first date.

The girls used to get loads of attention from the lads, which the girls loved, and it used to brighten up the lads' mornings as well as ours, so it worked all around! (Of course, times have changed with marriage and fatherhood – we each have two kids. We tend to treat the line between work and non-work as quite fuzzy; it's what happens when you are passionate about something. That can be a good thing when you're single and getting a business off the ground. But when you have a family, from your partner's perspective it can be viewed as not so good! We're still working on that!)

Even with its new fluorescent frontage, the Happy Pear was still a run-of-the-mill greengrocer's. Like most greengrocers in any town in Ireland, the main customers were busy mums and auld dears, the grannies! We figured that the mums were all too preoccupied for our food revolution and, no disrespect, but a food revolution with only the grannies just wasn't going to cut it – you need young people to start any sort of revolution! So we decided to glam things up and we installed a juice bar. (The first bar we built was from rough wood and Health and Safety came in and we had to re-do it all – one of our many mistakes!) The juice bar took off and attracted lots of younger people. It succeeded in adding a sexy element to our place and drew in more people with whom we could share our enthusiasm for healthy living.

About six months into our venture, the lease next door came up for sale and we thought, 'Why not? It will give us more room.' We decided to start a vegetarian café/restaurant. We simply wanted to showcase just how good healthy food could be. Again, we started the café with no experience. We had once washed pots in a restaurant when we were 15. That was the extent of our knowledge. Somehow it worked out.

Early on we tried anarchy as a style of management – like, really giving it a proper go for the best part of a year. We were all about equality and having a flat organizational structure so that everyone had equal rights to do what they wanted and add their creative input when they wanted. (This was back when we were still long-haired,

LEAVING THINGS better than we found them
EMBRACE MISTAKES
Healthy Eating
LOVE WHAT YOU ARE DOING
follow your dreams
HAPPY PEAR TREE by JACKIE BATES

trinket-wearing idealists fresh from our travels.) We only employed our friends in the early days, so this worked fine up to a point as they took their lead from us, but as more new people joined the team it turned into chaos and there came a point when we had to put more structure on how things were done. It then became 'all animals are equal but some are more equal than others'!

Having said that, we still don't have a very formal approach to business. We tend to make most decisions from our gut. This strategy often leads us back to one of our other strengths: embracing mistakes! We always just get back up on the horse as soon as we fall off. We love the Niels Bohr quote, 'An expert is a person who has made all the mistakes that can be made in a very narrow field.' By embracing mistakes and putting fear aside, we have more fun and live what we believe to be true by just going for it and not being too concerned about the outcome. Joking aside, you can analyse data till you're blue in the face, but like most people we tend to use the data to justify what our gut tells us anyway! Thankfully we are not worriers at all. We think the fact that we're twins and have such a strong rapport gives us much more security than if one of us was in a business on his own.

We defo think that our passion has been really important to getting us through our first ten years. The old saying of 'follow your dreams' is as true today as ever and that is what it boils down to for us. In our case, once we just went for it and took the leap into the unknown, life somehow supported us in ways in which we wouldn't have believed till we actually did it. People just showed up when we needed them and things just had a knack of sorting themselves out. Not to say that there hasn't been tonnes of hard work, but if you are fired up and love what you are doing then it is a hell of a lot easier to make it through the challenging times.

In our experience money has never been a real motivator – as long as we had enough to pay our rent, bills and staff, and go to the cinema every now and then, we were grand. For us there needs to be a sense of mission, something we're aiming towards.

At the heart of what the Happy Pear is about is leaving things better than we found them. And we want to make healthy eating mainstream! Society's attitude towards health has changed massively since we started. Nowadays it is nearly cool to be into health, to be a bit more conscious of what you put in your body. This probably stems from Hollywood actors and celebrities adopting healthier lifestyles, as it helps them look and feel better and to age slower. We figure that if a brown sugary carbonated drink can be cool, hip and sexy then surely fruit and veg – in all their amazing colours, curvy shapes and sizes – should defo be cool!

There is often this fuzzy idea with running an ethical business that you are a charity and odds-on you will go bankrupt due to inefficiencies from being too nice and not having enough backbone. But we have found that running an ethical business makes good financial sense. It makes financial sense BECAUSE of maintaining

integrity, not despite it. It is really basic: the more the business looks after all the parties involved – suppliers, employees, customers and the greater community – the more likely they are to look after you and support your business and talk it up to their friends.

Business is really about forming long-term relationships with customers, and what are long-term relationships based on? TRUST! Nowadays businesses have to be genuine and they have to do what they say they do, otherwise trust is lost. Customers will always hold you accountable and will give you many opportunities to be genuine or not. Trust may be lost over time, little by little, and customers may not know exactly why they stopped supporting your business, but they could simply be acting on a gut feeling that something was not quite right.

So we have found that really caring about all those we interact with – treating our suppliers how we want to be treated and paying them on time; offering delivery guys coffee or soup; really wanting the best for our staff, and genuinely wanting to better our community – is at the heart of our business. And it all makes good business sense too!

The other thing we care about is the planet and we've tried to be as green as possible. In 2011 we were very proud to be named the Greenest Retailer in Ireland (up against some of the biggest retail businesses in the country) in the annual Green Awards. We recycle all our plastic. All our green waste is composted. Much of our food waste is collected by a local pig man to feed his pigs. We use electricity from wind turbines. We had a van that ran on local vegetable oil and we hope to have gas vehicles soon that one day will run on compressed local biogas. We support local producers and love to barter with local growers in summer and autumn when they have a glut of something or other. We are doing our best!

A few years into starting the shop, we wanted to get Mum and Dad something to share our passion for health and to say thanks for their support. We got them a trip to Hippocrates Health Institute in Florida. It is a centre for treating disease by building up the immune system with the most nurturing and healthiest foods there are – sprouts, wheatgrass juice and green juices. It has a remarkable success rate in healing people from all kinds of sicknesses, such as many forms of cancer. The cornerstone of the programme is sprouts and wheatgrass.

After this trip, the family was very excited about having more of these foods available for ourselves and for others. Right away, Dad and our younger brother Darragh got to work on coming up with a location for producing these in Ireland. Within six months, in early 2009, the place we call 'Sproutville', in Newcastle, Co. Wicklow, just up the road from the shop, was up and running.

Darragh is the purest of the brothers, gentle and shiny. Animals always like Darragh the best: he is the type of guy whose leg a squirrel would choose to climb so it could get up and sit on his shoulder! He has time for everyone. Darragh was always into nature and growing things, and when we were starting the shop he got really into juicing, growing wheatgrass and sprouting for himself. When he felt the changes it made to his health, he wanted to share it with as many people as he could. So running the farm was a perfect fit for him.

Darragh began growing wheatgrass and sprouts for the shop initially. As time went on, he began refining and adding to the range of sprouted superfoods. In late 2011 Darragh, working with our wonderful Happy Pear pesto recipes, began to produce and distribute them to a few different outlets around Dublin. They were an immediate hit. As soon as people tried them, the great taste had them looking for more. We have continued to refine our recipes and improve our production methods, and following the success of the pestos, we look forward to releasing new Happy Pear products very soon.

Darragh is now head of all farming production and distribution. Today, the Happy Pear, under his management, distributes our wheatgrass, sprouts and pestos to around 75 outlets country-wide, though mainly in the greater Dublin area.

From the beginning, the thrust of this part of the business has been to make these incredibly healing and healthy foods more available and widespread for people. Education has been a huge part of this work. Talks, events, tastings and working with people and groups who share this vision have been fundamental for spreading this message. Thankfully, there are more and more people becoming aware of the benefits of eating living and sprouted foods for their health.

Wheatgrass is the young plant of wheat (the same wheat that's used to produce flour for bread), usually between 10 and 14 days old. Because it is harvested so young it has no gluten and is suitable for coeliacs. We have to juice wheatgrass because it's so fibrous that human stomachs can't properly digest it. (You need a masticating juicer to juice it; these range in price from a manual hand-crank one for €35 up to €5,000! We usually juice it with fresh ginger, lemon or lemongrass.) Nutritionally a shot of wheatgrass juice (same size as a regular shot in a pub, except very different effects!) is equal to one kilo of green veg in everything except fibre. It has every vitamin, 97 out of the 102 minerals, and is the greatest source of chlorophyll of any land-based plant (seaweeds and algae have higher amounts). Chlorophyll is considered to be nature's greatest blood cleanser and as a result wheatgrass is all about cleansing and detoxing. In the blood, chlorophyll is nearly identical to haemoglobin (which transports oxygen around your body), so it's a great boost to your immune system and energy production.

The summer of 2013 saw a new farming venture for us. We partnered with a local farm in Wicklow and took over the running of an amazing cherry and plum farm. It was a real FUN experience and the splendid summer weather helped produce a bumper crop. The fruit was incredible – mouth-watering and sweet. People everywhere were amazed that this was Irish fruit. Darragh heard phrases like, 'Really, this is Irish? It looks French or Turkish – wow!' These kind of reactions made all the work worthwhile. We had a lot of fun and it worked for both sides, so we are looking forward to a fruitful relationship growing into the future.

Today, ten years into our adventure, the Happy Pear consists of many more elements than the simple greengrocer's that we started with. Earlier in the book we introduced our chefs but we also have a fantastic team of innovators and creatives. We have more than fifty employees between the farm, the online shop, the online Happy Heart course, our food production, the shop and café on the main street in Greystones and our café in Shoreline, Greystones. Down the line, Darragh is confident that we will be growing more organic veg and developing into more farming and production. No matter what happens, fruit and veg will always be at the heart of all that we do.

# WATCH THIS SPACE – AND LONG LIVE THE WHOLEFOOD AND VEG REVOLUTION!

# THE HAPPY PEAR TOOLKIT

At the heart of what we do, we simply want to encourage you to eat more veg. Often people eat with us regularly, even for months, and don't notice that they're eating vegetarian food. It's just simple, tasty, wholesome food that happens to be vegetable based.

Each recipe in our book has been tried and tested on Happy Pear customers, then tweaked and improved until it's as good as possible. There are certain ingredients, tips and techniques that are the backbone of our way of cooking, so rather than repeat them in each recipe, here we'll guide you through them. We've listed things in alphabetical order. Though some of the products included here may be new to you, and you won't see all of them on the shelves of the supermarket, we promise that they are widely available in most health food shops, Asian shops or online. We don't use anything that you can't easily source.

## AUBERGINES

To many people, aubergines are *blah*, as they are used to eating them under-cooked and rubbery! But coated with a little oil and salt and baked in the oven for half an hour they come out golden and crispy and their centre becomes gooey and almost butter-like.

## BEANSPROUTS

Beansprouts are the white sprouted tails of mung beans. They are a lovely crunchy addition to a salad but not as nutritious as other sprouts (see page 228). After rinsing beansprouts, dry them well in a salad spinner – they go off quickly if they get soggy.

## AVOCADOS

Avocados are full of fantastic fatty loveliness, healthy fats that are good for your skin, hair and joints and may even help speed up your metabolism. They enhance any dish, and there is nothing like a ripe avocado as a bonus veg alongside your dinner. Picking ripe avocados can be an art form. Look for ones that are soft at the tip. They should not have any cavities or bruises and should feel like a tomato in terms of 'give' – neither too soft nor too firm. To help hard avocados ripen, put them into a brown bag with some bananas and leave in a warm place.

## BOUQUET GARNI

A small bunch of herbs added to a dish at the start of cooking and removed before serving. In ours we use thyme, rosemary, bay leaf and parsley. Wrap the bay leaf around the sprigs of the other herbs and tie together tightly with string. Using a bouquet garni imparts lovely herby flavours. Remember to remove it at the end of cooking, before serving!

## CACAO V. COCOA

The stuff that makes chocolate. They're basically the same thing, but cacao is produced at a lower temperature than cocoa so it's even more nutritious. Cocoa is great and you'll get it everywhere. Because it's closer to its natural state, we use cacao in our raw recipes. But don't stress about it: cacao/cocoa – it's all good!

## CHEESE

Nowadays most cheeses are made with vegetarian rennet. (Rennet is a bunch of enzymes used to coagulate the milk. If non-veggie, these enzymes come from the stomach of cattle. If veggie, a plant such as nettle is used.) However, Parmesan is always made with animal rennet and not suitable for vegetarians. Where we refer to veggie Parmesan, we usually use Gran Moravia, but just as often we use Wicklow Gold, a mature local Cheddar.

## COCONUT MILK

Immediately adds a rich, substantial component to any soup, stew or curry. We use it as a base for many of our curries. Chill a can for 8 hours. Pour off the clear liquid and whip up the rest with a little sweetener and vanilla extract to make a delicious non-dairy cream. If you are concerned about calories, low-fat coconut milk is typically around 10% in fat with fewer calories.

## BRAGG LIQUID AMINOS

A condiment that gives a nice salty depth to a dish. It's an American-type soy sauce that has not been fermented and has all eight essential amino acids (the components that make up protein). While we use tamari (see below) in the café/restaurant, we tend to use Bragg's at home. Like tamari, Bragg's has less sodium than soy sauce and it tastes great too – sweeter, smoother and more balanced than soy sauce.

## BREAD SODA/BAKING SODA/ BICARBONATE OF SODA

These are the same thing. Bread soda or baking soda are the more common names in Ireland.

## DATES

Super for making sweet treats. Moist and luxurious Medjool dates are the crème de la crème of the date world, but if you can't locate them, regular pitted dates are absolutely fine. In many of our dessert recipes we blend dates to a paste; if using standard pitted dates just add a little water when blending, to reach a nice thick caramel texture. Yum!

## EQUIPMENT

We mainly use a decent chef's knife (one with a good-size blade of about 20cm, with a wide base) and a serrated knife, which is ideal for tomatoes, peppers, aubergines, leeks, onions and most veg really. The chef's knife, if sharp, is good for pumpkins and harder veg; if very sharp it's great at cutting most veg. (Hint: maybe treat yourself to a knife sharpener!) Most large knives do not stay sharp for very long unless you're diligent about sharpening, so a serrated fellow is handier for lots of things.

Apart from that, the following will help, though none are essential:

- Food processor/blender – one of these makes life easier.
- Stick blender (soup gun) for blending soups, sauces, etc. while still in the pan or bowl – very worthwhile.
- Oven thermometer – a great way to see if your oven is true; a decent one costs less than €15.
- A pestle and mortar or coffee grinder.

- Juicer – there are two types: the most practical one to use, and the most common, is a centrifugal juicer and you can pick up a decent one of these for about €100. The key things to watch out for are a wide feeding tube – big enough to take a full apple at a time – and not too many bits to clean. Masticating juicers 'chew' the fruit or veg (just like your teeth), so they're slower and the quality of the juice is better, but they take more time to use and clean and are generally a little trickier. If you're new to juicing, we recommend starting with a centrifugal juicer.

## GARLIC

Crush it super-easy through a garlic press or with a pestle and mortar. If you have neither to hand, simply put a pinch of salt on your chopping board, put a peeled clove of garlic on top and squash it with the flat side of your knife blade till it splats. Continue to 'drag' your knife across the garlic and the salt will help to break it down into a paste.

## GINGER

This zingy root is great for digestion, for calming upset tummies including PMS and motion sickness, and adds fantastic flavour to any fresh juice, curry or Asian dish. We peel it, then grate it into dishes, or, if we can't find a grater, simply chop it finely or pound it in a pestle and mortar. Ginger lasts in the fridge for up to three weeks.

## GLUTEN-FREE COOKING

Nearly 90% of the recipes in this book are gluten-free (including most of our dessert section). We use an organic white spelt flour in most of our baking. It has low rather than no gluten, but that is usually fine for those who are gluten intolerant, though not for coeliacs. There are loads of gluten-free flours out there – rice, chickpea, almond, buckwheat (gluten-free though the name suggests otherwise) – and if you are a coeliac you will know them. Doves Farm gluten-free flour is widely available.

## LEEKS

One of our top five veg! In Spain they use only the green part of the leek, whereas in Ireland we use only the white. The green is the most nutritious part, and cooks down just like the white, so we use it all! We like to steam it or bake it with honey, salt and a splash of balsamic. Cooking it in a pan works great too.

To prepare a leek, give it a good wash by pulling the outer leaves right back and washing into the middle. Best to use a serrated knife to slice it. We typically cut it into small rounds right the way up.

## KALE

Kale is the king of veg in terms of nutrition. It comes in many shapes and sizes, with our favourite being cavalo nero/black Russian/dinosaur kale. Kale is a great veg to add to soups, to serve steamed as a side with some lemon and salt or as a powerful addition to any stew you make.

## MARGARINE

Nowadays many people have negative associations with margarine, but bear with us! In a couple of our cake recipes we use a plant-based solid fat a.k.a. margarine (Suma Sunflower Spread) instead of butter to make the cake dairy-free and more inclusive – this is the only reason.

## MILK – NON-DAIRY ALTERNATIVES

Rice, soya, oat, almond, hazelnut, coconut, quinoa – there is a huge selection of non-dairy milk options today. We love rice milk for porridge and for cereal – it's light and sweet and creamy. Oat is usually the most neutral taste and probably one of the most nutritious of these. Soya, oat and almond milk froth the best if you are a latte/cappuccino drinker. Most are below 10% in fat and often come enriched with other vitamins.

## NUT BUTTERS

We love nut butters! They go great in lots of desserts as a binder and an enricher. They are delicious in snacks – on crackers or toast – and we love to eat fruit dipped in nut butters.

## OIL

Stand by, as we're about to get controversial! We use oil in many dishes, as it makes things taste good, but, in our eyes, as oil is 100% fat, has no fibre and offers very little in terms of vitamins and minerals, it is a total junk food. This probably sounds like blasphemy (particularly if you are Spanish or Italian and love olive oil), but this is our two cents' worth.

There is lots of hype that coconut oil is the best for frying, as it holds its molecular structure longer at high temperatures, or that rapeseed and olive oils are 'heart healthy', etc. We are not believers in this. If you want to lose weight or you have high cholesterol or you are a high risk for a heart attack, excluding oil or greatly reducing your intake is worth considering.

In most of our mains recipes we don't specify what oil to use, as we think it doesn't really matter. Sunflower, olive, canola, coconut, whatever. Use whichever oil you're into or have to hand.

For salad dressings, we tend to use half neutral-tasting refined sunflower oil and half unrefined cold-pressed olive oil. If we only use a high-quality olive oil the taste is often too strong and can dominate everything else.

In making pestos, use olive oil if you like the taste, but a basic sunflower oil will be more neutral and you may be pleasantly surprised by the complexity of the flavour of your pesto.

## OVEN TEMPERATURES

All the electric oven temperatures given in our recipes are for a conventional oven. If using a fan oven, decrease them by 20°C/35°F.

## PAK CHOI (OR BOK CHOI)

Pak choi is a hard hitter in terms of nutrition, the fourth highest-ranking food pound per pound on Dr Joel Fuhrman's well-regarded Aggregate Nutrient Density Index (ANDI), behind only kale, watercress and collard greens. Pak choi is a gem, lovely crunchy fresh white stalks with tender leaves. It has a subtle taste and is not bitter like lots of greens. We like to juice it and, chopped and added towards the end, it adds great freshness to curries and stews.

## PEELING VEG

As most of the nutrition in veg is in or under the skin, we avoid peeling veg when we can. So when a vegetable is unpeeled in a recipe, that's deliberate. We spell it out when something should be peeled.

## PUMPKINS

Most people only know of pumpkins as something you carve for Hallowe'en, but those pumpkins are grown for size and are full of water and flavourless. In comparison, the pumpkins we use are small – green and orange fellas and really tasty! The green ones are often called kabocha squash and the orange ones either potimarron or hokkaido squash. But there are so many varieties. In September, when the first kabocha squashes show up, Dave can often be found eating a bowl of baked pumpkin for brekkie! In season they are incredible – really sweet and almost eggy-tasting, with a bright vibrant yellow colour that pimps up any dish.

To chop a pumpkin it's best to use a chef's knife or something with a large blade where you can get some leverage. Often, with large pumpkins, a good forceful chop from a reasonable height will split it in two. Then remove the seeds, turn each half face down so that the skin is facing up, chop it into half-moons, then stack these half-moons and chop them into bite-size pieces. We nearly always bake our pumpkins if we have time, as it brings out even more sweetness. We eat them with the skin on. Leaving the skin on keeps the pumpkin from breaking up into mush, and it doesn't affect the flavour or the texture.

## QUINOA

A nutritional powerhouse! Rinse the tiny grains under cold water using a fine mesh strainer. Like rice, you cook quinoa by volume (in the ratio 2:1 liquid-to-grain), so once you've measured out the amount specified in the recipe, see how far up it comes in a mug or measuring jug before putting it into a medium size saucepan. Then, using the same mug or jug, measure out twice that volume of water or stock and add it to the quinoa with a pinch of salt. Bring to the boil, then reduce the heat to the lowest setting, cover, and cook till all the water is absorbed (about 15–20 minutes). Remove from the heat and leave to stand, still covered, for 5 minutes. You'll know it's ready when the grains have 'popped' and the germ is exposed.

## RICE

We always use brown rice. Due to its high fibre content, brown rice is a slow-release source of energy and has way more nutrition in it than white. There are two main types: brown basmati is a longer-grain rice which usually ends up fluffy and with the grains slightly separate; short-grain brown rice tastes nuttier and tends to be stickier. Brown basmati is more commonly available.

To cook, rinse the rice in cold water using a sieve. Put it in a saucepan and cover with at least twice the amount of water (by volume – so if you used a cup to measure out the rice, add 2 cups of water). Put the lid on and bring to the boil. Then turn the heat down to a gentle simmer and cook with the lid on till nearly all the water evaporates (about 30 minutes). Never let the pot dry out – if it does and the rice is not yet cooked, simply add more water. You will know that the rice is cooked when the grains are completely clear of any white dot. It should be soft and tender.

## SALT

We like salt! We think it is vital to any dish. It brings out the flavours and helps them come together. If you think a recipe might have too much salt for your palate, just add less than we suggest and check it. It's best to use an unrefined sea salt such as Irish Atlantic Sea Salt or Maldon.

## 'SAUTÉING' IN WATER

This is an amazingly effective technique that we use to cut fat in our Happy Heart recipes. Rather than starting off the veg in oil, you simply put them into a little water or stock. The trick is to cook everything down rapidly in the liquid so that eventually the veg are simmering in their own juices. If the veg start to stick, add a bit more liquid.

## SOUP

Making soup is an art form, but once you know how and understand a few simple things, there is usually no need to follow a recipe. You can very easily freestyle soup from what is in your cupboard and fridge!

At the base of all our soups are celeriac, carrot and onion. (Celeriac is a starchy root veg with subtle undertones of celery – great for adding body to a soup as well a slight celery flavour.) We chop all these roughly and cook them together until they're soft. Then we add whatever veg, beans and grains are the main signature of the soup, for example red pepper, lentils and chopped tomatoes or carrot, leek and cashew . . .

When we have time, we always bake our veg as it adds sweetness and concentrates the flavours.

Regarding texture, decide whether you want your soup to be chunky, thick or thin. Be wild and free – you can always recover! If it's too thin, add something starchy to thicken it, for example grate in a potato or blend in a tin of beans. If it's too thick, add more water/stock/coconut milk and re-season.

What makes the difference between a mediocre soup and a really good one is the seasoning. Here are a few things that we like to use to make our soups stand out:

- salt and pepper – seasoning 101, always the place to start!
- coconut milk – if a soup needs a drastic overhaul try adding coconut milk; there's nothing like extra fat to bring everything together
- pinch of chilli or cayenne
- ground cumin
- ground ginger
- harissa paste
- lemon juice
- sweetener – agave syrup or honey (often needed with tomato-based soups)
- tamari
- Thai curry paste

## SPICES AND HERBS

In typical French cooking flavour comes from fat such as cream and butter; in ours, the flavour comes from herbs and spices. While herbs are usually the leaves of plants, spices are everything else – the root (turmeric), fruit (chillies), seed (fennel), berry (allspice) or bark (cinnamon) of the plant. We use plenty of herbs and spices in our cooking, usually fresh ones, but we try not to use too many fresh herbs in any one recipe.

We hope that as you cook our recipes your spice arsenal will increase and you will start to familiarize yourself with many flavours and aromas. Here are our essentials:

- **cayenne** – very hot fella, use a pinch at a time
- **chilli** – fresh or ground; if using fresh the heat comes from the seeds, so remove them if you don't like it hot!
- **cinnamon** – quills or ground, both have their merits
- **coriander** – ground and whole seeds; make sure to finely grind if using the whole seeds
- **cumin** – ground and whole seeds – adds lovely musky depth to a dish
- **curry powder**
- **nutmeg** – nice in béchamel sauces
- **paprika** – dried and ground red pepper, adds a slight sweet taste and red colour
- **smoked paprika** – has a lovely smoked oaky taste

## SPRING ONIONS V. SCALLIONS

The terms are used interchangeably in Ireland, but there's a difference. Scallions are younger and don't have the developed bulbous white end that spring onions have. They are interchangeable in our recipes though: an average bunch of scallions (about 6–8) is the same as about 3–4 spring onions.

## SPROUTS

They might have a hippie image, but consider this: at the end of World War 2 the US government mounted a PR campaign to educate the public on how to sprout, as it was the easiest, most affordable and best way to ensure that they could access great nutrition!

Sprouts are the young shoots (3–12 days old) of seeds or beans such as alfalfa, broccoli, leek, beans, lentils, etc., and are in their nutritional prime. Gram for gram, they contain more nutrition than even the healthiest of green vegetables. These are living foods loaded with enzymes. Think of enzymes as your life-force – they are involved in every function in your body but are in finite supply, so it is important to eat foods high in enzymes. They are high in everything that's good for you. Most foods we eat nowadays are cooked or have been slowly decomposing and losing enzymes/vitality since they were harvested.

Sprouts come in many shapes, flavours, colours and sizes. Darragh (lord of the sprouts!) grows about 20 different types – mung and aduki beans, lentils, alfalfa, carrot, fennel, pea, leek, garlic,

SPROUTS ARE THE YOUNG SHOOTS OF SEEDS OR BEANS SUCH AS ALFALFA, BROCCOLI, LEEK, BEANS, LENTILS, ETC. GRAM FOR GRAM, THEY CONTAIN MORE NUTRITION THAN EVEN THE HEALTHIEST OF GREEN VEGETABLES.

broccoli, sunflower, clover, radish, to name just a few. If you can't see them in your local shop, sprouts are easy to grow, are a great addition to any salad and will really increase the nutritional bang you get from your salad.

## SWEETENERS

We avoid processed sugar but that doesn't mean we don't like a little sweetness in our lives – check out our legendary desserts! There are many healthier options when it comes to sweetening a dish, e.g. liquid sweeteners like honey or maple syrup. Agave syrup is a good alternative to honey if you're vegan. Coconut sugar is nutritious and safe for diabetics. Xylitol is also lower than sugar in calories and safer for diabetics. And of course, if it's more convenient, coconut sugar/xylitol in our recipes can be replaced by regular sugar.

## TAHINI

Tahini is like peanut butter made with sesame seeds instead of peanuts. It has a lovely, fatty, gooey consistency that sometimes gets caught on the roof of your mouth! We use it in hummus and in some dressings. Dave loves to dip apples or bananas in tahini as a snack. Smear it on toast or rice cakes with a drizzle of honey and you are elected (as our granny used to say!).

## TAMARI

Tamari adds a nice salty depth to a dish and we use it lots. We think tamari is much nicer than soy sauce. Soy sauces can be very sharp and a bit crude, whereas tamari is lower in sodium, usually gluten-free, and has a smoother and more complex flavour. (It is soy-based, so avoid if you're avoiding soy.) Go tamari!

## TEMPEH

A fermented soya bean block. Not a very appealing description, but when prepared right it tastes 'meaty' and substantial – *we love you, tempeh!* It is healthier than tofu, as it has more healthy bacteria, but is not as readily available (try the chill cabinets in Asian shops). Under 'tofu' below, see our fab marinade that also works for tempeh.

## TOFU

We see tofu as a blank canvas. It is really bland out of the packet, so it's what you do with it that makes it stand out. We like to bake it in a tamari-and-ginger-based marinade. In our cooking we only use hard tofu, which is usually available in the chill cabinets of most health food shops or supermarkets.

*Our favourite tofu and tempeh marinade:* 8 tablespoons tamari, 2 teaspoons ginger (chopped fresh or ground), 10 tablespoons orange juice, juice of a lime, a crushed clove of garlic, 1 tablespoon honey or agave, sometimes chilli or harissa, sometimes paprika, sometimes sesame oil. Sit a block of tofu or tempeh in this marinade for at least 30 minutes, then bake, still in the marinade, at 200°C/400°F/gas mark 6 for 30 minutes.

# INDEX

## A

almonds: chermoula and herb couscous 85

    chocolate almond recovery smoothie 24

    chocolate-coated 'caramel' bars 180

    fig rolls 191

    granola bars 192

    no-bake healthy brownies 198

    raw power bars 201

    roasted red pepper and almond cream sauce 139

    Vietnamese sweet almond curry 126

apples: beetroot, spinach, apple and toasted seed salad 77

    in veg juices 27

asparagus: spring frittata 30

aubergines 220

    aubergine, fennel and bean stew 113

    aubergine parmigiana 150

    Indonesian aubergine satay 116–17

    moussaka 144–5

    roasted Mediterranean veg and local Cheddar lasagne 148–9

    Sri Lankan veg curry 125

    Vietnamese sweet almond curry 126

avocados 220

    avocado chocolate mousse cake 176

    avocado and tomato toastie 38

    avocado-tastic smoothie 24

    black sesame, carrot and avocado salad 82

    guacamole 100

    with quinoa, butterbean and butternut squash burger 133

    zingy citrus cream 24

## B

bananas: banana and walnut cake 175

barley: shitake mushroom and pot barley broth 51

basil: mint and basil dressing 96

beans *see individual beans*

beansprouts 220

beetroot: beetroot, spinach, apple and toasted seed salad 77

    beetroot, walnut and feta burgers 130

    Dave's Thai red curry 121

    veggie detox juice 27

black beans: aubergine, fennel and bean stew 113

    Mexican leek and black bean chilli 114

    Vietnamese sweet almond curry 126

bok choi *see* pak choi

bouquet garni 220

Bragg liquid aminos 221

bread: Claire's stuffed flatbreads 41

    rye sourdough bread 36–7

    wholemeal spelt bread 38

broccoli: Asian broccoli salad in a sweet chilli sauce 79

    broccoli, sweet potato and ginger soup 54

    Sri Lankan veg curry 125

    white lasagne 142–3

brownies 198

burgers: beetroot, walnut and feta burgers 130

    quinoa, butterbean and butternut squash burger 133

butter beans: hearty Italian veg and white bean soup 47

    quinoa, butterbean and butternut squash burger 133

butternut squash: quinoa, butterbean and butternut squash burger 133

    Vietnamese sweet almond curry 126

# C

# THANKS!

A huge amount of work has gone into our first book, which has been ten years in the making. We are indebted to the many dedicated and talented people who helped make it happen.

First, thanks to our families for putting up with all the late-night writing and recipe testing that has gone on – you have been very understanding and supportive: Janet, Justyna, May, Elsie, Theo and Izzy.

Thanks to Dad and Mum – Donal and Ismay – for tasting lots of the dishes, and to Dad for your eye for detail. Dar, thanks for doing all the dips, and Mark, thanks for having a look from a distance!

Thanks to Yeşim for all your help with the writing and for your great eye for detail and your lovely calm demeanour!

We are indebted to our great chefs, who are all integral to what we do and have been central to the book. Phil and Dorene both contributed quite a few recipes. You are both fantastic and such an asset to the Happy Pear and to the two of us – thank you. Thanks, Claire, for your great enthusiasm for the book right from the start: thanks for contributing recipes and for your amazing and very inspiring creativity. Thanks to Michelle (Shel) Hunt for your brilliant dessert recipes – you are brill at what you do and are another invaluable asset to the Happy Pear team. He Qiang, thanks for the salads and for always being so diligent in saying 'yes' when we come looking for help. Our wonderful baking team of Jen, Ola and Emily: thanks for all your patience and commitment. You are all fantastic and brilliant at what you do and we are lucky to have such competent bakers.

Thanks to all the great recipe testers who helped us tweak and refine these recipes in their intended environment – people's home kitchens! Thanks to Ann Marie Burke, who trialled lots of recipes and had a great input. Thanks to John Hartnett, Sinead and Rory, Gerry, to all the Bourke Barnwells: Helen, Paddy, Anna, Morgan, Hectus and Marny. Thanks to Helen and Brian, to handsome Matt for his great palate, enthusiasm and support. Thanks to Danica Murphy for her fantastic eye for detail and great enthusiasm for trialling recipes.

Thanks to our agents, Faith O'Grady and Eavan Kenny, for getting the whole process started and for introducing us to Penguin.

At Penguin, thanks to our wonderful editor, Patricia Deevy, for caring so much and driving this project on with as much gusto as we have. You have been a pleasure to work with and your experience has been invaluable.

Thanks to the lovely Sarah Fraser for her great eye and her capacity for making things look beautiful. Your design work has been central too. Thanks to all your team – Gail Jones, Gillian Heeley, Alison O'Toole and the rest of the gang. And thanks to John Hamilton for believing in the book. Also at 80 Strand, thanks to James Blackman, Sara Granger, Keith Taylor and Nicky Palmer, who were early believers too and worked so hard to help make it happen.

Thanks to Alistair Richardson for the lovely photography and great work ethic: we really admire and appreciate your professionalism. Thanks also to Alan Rowlette for taking some great additional photographs when we realized we had missed a few. Thanks to Laura George, Monique McQuaid, Claire Brennan, Mary B. Deevy, Joni, Joe and Terry for lending us such beautiful props.

Thanks to Annie Lee for all her top-class copy-editing. We have called you Eagle Eyed Annie for your wonderful attention to detail!

Thanks to Tamsin English for getting the ball rolling. This book would not have happened without your belief, support and encouragement. Thank you. We love you dearly!

Thanks to all our great staff at the Happy Pear, as without you guys we wouldn't have a business. Thanks for caring so much and for making the journey great fun. Thanks to Symon for doing such a great job running the farm. Thanks to Alan Smith for his guidance and support with all things branding, and more, over the years. And thanks to all our lovely suppliers – you have all been central to our story too.

Finally, thanks to the people of Greystones and beyond – without your support none of this would ever have happened!